# LEXICOGRAPHY IN AFRICA

## PROGRESS REPORTS FROM THE DICTIONARY RESEARCH CENTRE WORKSHOP AT EXETER, 24 - 25 MARCH 1989

edited by

R. R. K. Hartmann



Volume 15

EXETER LINGUISTIC STUDIES

General Editor: R. R. K. Hartmann

University of Exeter Press 1990

First published 1990 by University of Exeter Press
Printed in Great Britain by BPCC Wheatons Ltd, Exeter
ISBN 085989 3456

## TABLE OF CONTENTS

## Preface

One of the special events marking the fifth anniversary of the Dictionary Research Centre was the Workshop on Lexicography in Africa, which arose out of the fortuitous presence of several African scholars at Exeter during the 1988-89 session. Of these, Mairo Kidda Awak from Nigeria and Masidake Busane from Zaïre shared enthusiastically in the preparatory work. Of those reading papers, Michael Mann (SOAS, London) freely gave of his encyclopedic knowledge about African languages and cultures and imposed his quiet authority on the lively discussions. The participants are listed at the end of the book; Rufus Gouws willingly accepted our invitation to submit an additional paper on Southern Africa to complete the picture. We also had the benefit of looking at preliminary drafts of articles for the international encyclopedia *Wörterbücher/Dictionaries/Dictionnaires* by John Haywood, Hans Heestermans, Paul and Roxana Newman, and Edgar Polomé (see Bibliography, Section 8.3).

I gratefully acknowledge the help of all authors of papers and state-of-the-art reports, of Exeter University's conference and library staff, and of the British Council for sponsoring 3 participants. Special thanks are due to Avril Smith who prepared camera-ready copy, and to Karen Pancer who assisted with proof-reading

What emerges is the first tentative conspectus of lexicography in Africa, with all its exciting possibilities and external constraints. We hope that this volume can make a modest contribution to the beginning international debate on dictionary research in that vast and interesting continent. We dedicate it to the memory of Robert Collison (d.10/4/1989) who did so much to raise the level of awareness about both lexicography and Africa.

Reinhard Hartmann
Exeter, April 1990

# 1 A linguistic map of Africa

by Michael Mann

*Introduction*

Estimates of the number of languages spoken in Africa seem to climb inexorably upwards. Alexandre (1972: 2) put the total at about 800, while acknowledging other estimates of 1200; Mann & Dalby (1987) enumerate 2550. In part these differing figures reflect different definitions of language, emphasising communicability (Alexandre) or identity (Mann & Dalby). But they also reflect the limits of knowledge: again and again closer examination of an area discloses the over-simplification of previous reports. Nor is the linguistic situation static, though there have been surprisingly few reports of languages actually dying out; rather, the dramatic reports are of growth in *lingua francas* which people acquire in addition to their home language.

The conflicting pressures of inter-communication (tending to bring languages together) and of preservation of identity (tending to preserve distance between languages) yield a certain equilibrium, as has been observed in studies of dialect in Europe (Séguy 1971). There are extreme cases where lack of communication in isolated communities such as the San (Bushmen) of Southern Africa leads to strong linguistic differentiation, or where the lack of any large identity leads to a linguistic continuum, with language changing by slow degrees as one moves from village to village, as among the Kru of the Ivory Coast and Liberia, or the Bamileke of Cameroon (traditionally stateless societies). More commonly, a broadly static linguistic equilibrium yields slowly to changing patterns of society, such as urbanisation, migrant labour and longer distance communication, and is relatively resistant to any form of government planning.

It is a striking fact that many of the well-known language-names of modern Africa are of recent origin. Koelle (1854), reporting from Sierra Leone in the mid-nineteenth century, attacks both "Ibo" and "Yoruba" as names improperly imposed on a diversity of peoples:

> In Sierra Leone certain natives who have come from the Bight are called Ibos. In speaking to some of them respecting this name, I learned that

> they never heard it till they came to Sierra Leone. In their own country they seem to ... know only the names of their respective districts or countries.
>
> Aku, or rather ˊỌku, is a mode of salutation among all the tribes enumerated ... and hence all of them are designated in Sierra Leone "Akus", not only by Europeans, but also and chiefly by the native population. It is consequently not the historical name by which these various tribes are united in one nation, but is here retained because the historical name is not known at present ... For the last few years [the missionaries] have very erroneously made use of the name "Yórūba" in reference to the whole nation, supposing that the Yórūban is the most powerful Aku tribe. But this appellation is liable to far greater objections than that of Aku, and ought to be forthwith abandoned... If, *e.g.*, you call an Idṣẹ́buan or a Yắgban a Yórūban, he will always tell you, "Don't call me by that name, I am not a Yórūban;" just, *e.g.*, as the Wúrtembergians or Bavarians would never suffer themselves to be called Prussians.

Modern Yoruba and Igbo are "standard" forms based on the speech of Oyo and Onitsha, co-existing with local forms of speech, though not without controversy, particularly in the case of Igbo.

In a similar way Shona stems from a government report (Doke 1931) offering an amalgam of three "dialects" (Manyika, Karanga, Zezuru) out of the six related dialects that the author distinguished in Zimbabwe. (Examination of the comparative vocabulary appended to the report from some 30 "Shona"-speaking centres shows that the distinction of only six "dialects" was already greatly simplistic). The modern STANDARD SHONA DICTIONARY (Hannan 1984) still distinguishes the dialectal provenance of words.

On the other hand many well-known languages owe their establishment to political entities pre-dating the colonial period. One such case is luGanda, the product of the dynasty of Buganda founded in the 15th century. In some cases such historical origins separate languages that are so close linguistically as to be inter-intelligible, for example kiRundi and kinyaRwanda, which owe their distinct identities to traditional kingdoms and now to the modern states of Burundi and Ruanda.

*Languages with over 1 million speakers*

Attempts to count or enumerate the major languages of Africa – say those having more than 1 million speakers – run into numerous ambiguities and uncertainties. Population estimates are uncertain and never up-to-date. One language name may cover a population speaking diverse dialects that may be barely interintelligible. Or a large population speaking highly similar dialects may regard itself as so many groups each with their own language – as for instance the Nguni peoples speaking siZulu, siXhosa, siSwati and siNdebele, or in Europe the Swedes and the Danes. And finally does one count the number who speak a language at home ("speakers"), or also those who may understand it and use it in transactions outside the home (we might call them "hearers", to adopt a West African usage).

The map (Figure 1) and accompanying table (Table 1) represent languages currently spoken by more than 1 million; estimates have been based on the proportion of the national population speaking each language (taken from Mann & Dalby 1987) combined with recent national population estimates (as reported in Appendix A); this assumes a roughly proportional growth in numbers of speakers, which is not too unreasonable, but the growth in the number of "hearers" of second languages may well be in excess of population growth (one language narrowly excluded by these criteria, but which may well have more than 1 million hearers, is Soso, the language of Conakry, capital of Guinée).

Of these 85 languages, 35 are Bantu languages; the Bantu languages, occupying most of Africa South of the Equator, are a strikingly close-knit family of languages, plausibly owing their origin (or at least the origin of those spoken outside the equatorial forest) to a rapid expansion from the North-East starting some 2000 years ago, assisted by the new technology of iron and cereal agriculture. Their similarities of grammar and vocabulary are broadly comparable with those among the Germanic languages (common origin about 1600 years ago) or the Slavonic languages (1100 years). The Bantu languages are part of a much larger group of languages, which Greenberg has called Niger-Congo (or, with the addition of some languages of the Sudan, Niger-Kordofanian); however, while the ultimate historical relatedness of these languages is generally accepted, the relationship is often remote, and seems more like reminiscences than resemblances. Afroasiatic is again a large and remote language grouping, within which are included the Semitic languages: Arabic has

Figure 1: major languages of Africa, spoken or understood by 1 million or more

Language names indicate as nearly as possible the location and extent of languages; where smaller type is used, names may extend beyond their true area or be slightly displaced. Italics indicate the area over which a language is understood as a second language.

a single standard written form, but the spoken language varies widely from place to place; Amharic is the official language of Ethiopia, with its own script, which is also used for other languages of Ethiopia. Nilo-Saharan is the name given to a group whose historical unity is less certain, though both Luo and Dinka belong to the narrower Nilotic group. There are no representatives of Greenberg's fourth language phylum, the Khoisan, in the table, the largest group, the Nama, numbering only some 120,000.

| *Bantu* | ciBemba | Mandinka–Bambara | *Afroasiatic* | *Nilo-Saharan* |
|---|---|---|---|---|
| ┌ Ewondo | chiChewa–chiNyanja | Soninke | Arabic | Songhai |
| └ Fang | ciSena | Mende | Amharic | Kanuri |
| Kongo | Shona | Kpelle | Tigrinya | Sara |
| Lingala | ┌ seTswana | | | Dinka |
| ciLuba | │ sePedi | Moore | Berber: | Nuer |
| kiLuba | └ seSotho | Sena | ┌ Qabayil | Luo |
| kiMbundu | Tsonga | | └ Tamazight | Kalenjin |
| uMbundu | ┌ siNdebele | Baule | | Teso |
| ┌ ruNyankore | │ siSwati | ┌ Twi | Beja | Lwoo |
| └ ruChiga | │ siZulu | └ Fante | Somali | ┌ Acholi |
| ┌ kinyaRwanda | └ siXhosa | Ewe | Oromo | └ Lango |
| └ kiRundi | | Fon | Hadiya | |
| luGanda | *Other Niger-Congo* | Yoruba | Sidamo | *Malayo-Polynesian:* |
| Luhya | | Edo | | Malagasy |
| kiGusii | Serer | Nupe | Welaita | |
| Gikuyu | Wolof | Igbo | | |
| kiKamba | Pulaar-Fulfulde | Efik-Ibibio | Hausa | *Indo-European:* |
| kiMeru | Temne | Tiv | | Afrikaans |
| Sukuma | | | | English |
| kiSwahili | | Ijo | | Pijin |
| Yao | | Sango | | |
| eMakua | | Gbaya | | |
| Makonde | | | | |

Table 1: major languages of Africa, by linguistic group
(languages considered intercomprehensible are bracketed together)

## *Language functions*

The great majority of African states south of the Sahara have as language of administration and post-elementary education the language of the former colonial power, although these languages are in general known to only some 10–20% of the population. The most notable exceptions are Tanzania, where the adoption of kiSwahili and a vigorous adult education programme has led to a claimed 85% literacy rate in kiSwahili, and Somalia, where Somali is used for all public business and for education to tertiary level (following the introduction of the policy in 1972, public servants were given three months to learn the new writing system for Somali, or face dismissal). Reasons for the state of affairs elsewhere are sometimes pragmatic (the diversity of local languages), sometimes political (the promotion of national unity), but usually also reflecting notions of prestige derived from the colonial culture; in consequence African languages have been relatively neglected.

In an interesting paper, Heine (1977) distinguished between languages of vertical and horizontal communication in Africa. Vertical languages are typically official languages whose use is assertive of authority and social distance, while horizontal languages are socially neutral and symbolise social equality and solidarity. (A shopkeeper in Nairobi, for instance, might use kiSwahili in normal dealings, but switch to English in dealing with a customer who had defaulted on credit.) African languages are typically horizontal in this sense, and a number of observations have implications for African lexicography: horizontal languages are typically learned informally, while vertical languages are learned in school; they are mediated orally rather than through writing, and performance is judged by effective communication rather than "correctness". There is consequently often considerable local and individual variation within a language used horizontally, and vocabulary often grows or changes very rapidly.

| | | | | | |
|---|---|---|---|---|---|
| -:níiyá | -nzíiɲá | -:níiɲá | | | |
| -:níniiyá | -nzíziiɲá | | | | |
| -:nígiiyá | -nzígiiɲá | | | | |
| | -nzígiriɲá | | | | |
| | | | | | |
| -:núuyá | -nzúuɲá | | | | -:ɲúuyá |
| -:núnuuyá | -nzúzuuɲá | -:núnuuɲá | | | -:ɲúɲuuyá |
| | -nzúzuruɲá | | | | |
| | -nzúguuɲá | -:núguuɲá | | | |
| | -nzúguruɲá | -:núguruɲá | | -:ɲúguruɲá | |
| | | | | | |
| -:núuyú | -nzúuɲú | | -:núurú | | |
| -:núnuuyú | -nzúzuuɲú | | -:núnuurú | | -:ɲúɲuuyú |
| | -nzúzuruɲú | | | | |
| -:núguuyú | -nzúguuɲú | | -:núguurú | | |
| -:núguruyú | -nzúguruɲú | | | -:ɲúguruɲú | |

Table 2: words for "very small" in kinyaRwanda

Coupez (1975) reported another phenomenon of African languages that he likewise attributed to the oral medium and to the lack of the standardising pressures of a written form. There often exist lexical variants that are not distinguished in meaning and are almost the same in sound. Table 2 shows 35 words for "very small" in kinyaRwanda; these are not dialectal variants, but all forms that can be used at will by a single speaker. This phenomenon is not unique to Africa – traces can be seen in the English series *tiny, teeny, teeny-*

*weeny, tinsy-winsy, titchy* etc. – but is much more prevalent in Africa: I found 250 sets of phonologically related synonyms in kiSwahili, although usually with two or three words in each set. The question is rather why it is not more apparent elsewhere; Coupez concludes that it is written standardisation that has stifled the expressivity characteristic of spoken languages, and that is also apparent in the richness of ideophones in many African languages.

*Implications for lexicography*

The complexity revealed in the preceding paragraphs indicate the enormous task facing lexicographers in Africa. It will be seen in later pages that the principal focus of much existing lexicography is the foreign learner, and that very few languages have monolingual dictionaries or any form of linguistic work designed primarily for the mother-tongue speaker. The major languages distinguished above frequently represent not a single "lect" but a chain of inter-intelligible lects, that can with difficulty be served by a single dictionary. And the dynamic and rapidly developing nature of many African languages quickly causes dictionaries to become out of date. Perhaps the word-processing revolution, with the opportunities it presents for continual updating, will afford a timely tool in the service of African lexicography.

# 2 Historical Background, with Special Reference to Western Africa*

by Mairo Kidda Awak

*Introduction*

The dictionary-making industry has recently undergone considerable proliferation in terms of languages and subjects covered. The types of dictionaries have diversified from the purely conventional to thesaurus and even the more encyclopedic. Some are monolingual, others are bilingual or trilingual, while a few comprise more than three languages.

As regards the number of dictionaries, Quirk (1986) reports a collection of over 8,000 different types of dictionaries from all over the world in the library of Indiana State University at Terre Haute. (This is indeed one of the largest collections, and it is probable that this number has increased by 1989). Of this number, at least 6,700 are dictionaries of English, reflecting the fact that lexicographers have devoted more attention to this language than to any other. With such a proliferation of dictionaries, one finds it disheartening to realize that most languages of the world, particularly African languages, lack adequate lexical coverage.

This situation is rather unfortunate considering that long ago there existed in Africa some syllabic and ideographic forms of writing, e.g. the Vai and the Mende syllabaries in Liberia and Sierra Leone, and the Bamum (in the Cameroon) and Nsibidi (in Nigeria) ideographics, which could have developed into viable literary traditions that might have been used in reversing the trend. The Vai (a dialect of Mandingo) syllabary was invented in about 1829 (or possibly two centuries earlier,

*I wish to express my profound gratitude to the Association of Commonwealth Universities and the British Council for their financial and moral support during my research fellowship at Exeter. My thanks also go to the University of Exeter Dictionary Research Centre for its services, and particularly to its Director, Dr. R.R.K. Hartmann, for invaluable expert advice. Above all, I would like to thank the University of Maiduguri and the Vice-Chancellor, Professor Muhammad Mur Alkali, without whose support my valuable year in England would have been impossible.

as speculated), while the Mende (a related language) syllabary was devised in 1921. The Bamum and Nsibidi ideographic writings were created in about 1903 and 1930, respectively. Other languages such as Fula, Kpelle, Mandingo and Wolof had some forms of writing invented at about the same time or later (Diringer 1949, Dalby 1968). However, it must be noted that, although the signs of these scripts were known to many speakers of these languages, the knowledge of their symbolisms was, for religious or occultist reasons, limited to only certain groups.

In this paper, I attempt to examine, in relation to the African past and present experience, the scope of lexicography and highlight the problems and/or limitations of dictionary making, with particular reference to West Africa.

*The Scope of Lexicography*

An examination of the development of lexicography (and linguistics in general) in Africa reflects three major events: the Christian missions, colonial expansion and the development of modern linguistics and anthropology.

Christian missionaries had worked in parts of Africa since the sixteenth century, but their work intensified in the last quarter of the nineteenth century with the establishment of colonial rule. Depending on one's views, the presence of the missionaries in Africa may be seen as a response to a religious calling ('internalist view') or as a mere concomitant of the gradual implantation of a colonial regime ('externalist view'). Perhaps one can avoid the fruitless debate on the motives of Christian evangelization and better appreciate the practical and specific contributions made by the missionaries if their role is understood as having been crucial in pioneering lexicographical activities in Africa.

The missionaries were the first and most active in producing lexicons of African languages. (In this paper, the term 'lexicon' is used to include items that have been labelled as wordlists, vocabularies and dictionaries.) As Cole (1971) reports, during the period between 1643 and 1660, several works by Jesuit and Capuchin priests were produced; however, most of these were not published and can no longer be traced. Among them were a quadrilingual dictionary comprising Italian, Latin, Spanish and kiKongo by Brusciotto (1650), a kiKongo-Spanish dictionary by Antoine de Tervelli (1652) and a Latin-Spanish-kiKongo dictionary by Georges (1652). It is interesting to note that these early dictionaries involved only one African language, namely kiKongo (in Central Africa).

The nineteenth century witnessed a rapid increase in the number of African lexicons. More African languages were covered, particularly those in West Africa. However, most of these appear in the form of bilingual or polyglot vocabularies accompanied by grammar sketches. Prominent among these were Avezac's (1845) vocabulary of five languages (i.e. Fula, Mandingo, Sarakolé, Serer and Wolof); Clapperton's (1829) vocabulary of Hausa, Igbo, and Yoruba; Norris' (1841) outline of a vocabulary of a few West African languages (i.e. Bambara, Kanuri, Mande and Vai); Kilham's (1827) vocabularies of thirty African languages, mostly western, including, among others, Ashanti, Fula, Hausa, Igbo, Kanuri, Mandingo, Urhobo and Wolof; and Koelle's (1854) monumental POLYGLOTTA AFRICANA, consisting of 283 words and phrases in 156 languages, mostly of West Africa, as spoken by freed slaves settled in Freetown (for references to the above, cf. Meier 1984).

Although credit is to be given to these early works, it must be noted that:

> Except for a few, all the other vocabularies lack systematic arrangement. Some were collected to serve as conversation manuals for European sailors and traders, but are poorly organized: the majority were collected perhaps only as curiosities, funny words from a strange land. Finally, a sizeable proportion of the material comes merely in the form of single terms scattered through accounts of exploration or topography or commerce: almost all the very earliest material comes in this form. (Hair 1970:15)

This state of affairs is not surprising considering that these early vocabularies were not compiled for use by Africans. While some were meant to serve as expeditionary guides for the European explorers, others were produced to be used by the missionaries in learning the African languages for the purpose of evangelization. Indeed, Hall and Hall (1950:1), stating the objective for a Moore (Mossi) vocabulary, echo this view:

> The primary purpose of this vocabulary is to aid new missionaries to more rapidly acquire sufficient language for reading the New Testament in Moré and to preach and teach the Gospel which is so necessary to the salvation of Mossi souls.

The above fact notwithstanding for missionaries and non-missionaries alike, a consistent approach to the problem of devising orthographies was conspicuously absent, due to a general lack of understanding of the phonemic systems of the African languages. Often, this resulted in a language or related languages acquiring two or more orthographies. Alexandre (1961:70) cites an extreme example of this where Fang (an important language in Gabon) has acquired

> trois transcriptions [catholiques] et deux [protestantes] pour environ un million de locuteurs, sans parler des différences morphologiques dues à des calques catholiques, sur l'allemand, le français et l'espagnol, et protestants, sur l'américain.

Another related problem involves meaning representation. For instance, Hair (1970) reports the Portuguese discovering Portuguese words in African utterances; thus, the Temne word *ka-bonklo* 'bush-cat' (with shining eyes) became equated with the Portuguese *carbunclo* (carbuncle) 'precious stone', in reality a case of homophony!

The establishment of colonial rule gave a boost to missionary activities, as the missions were entrusted with educational tasks in the colonies. The missions also had a vested evangelical interest in ensuring that as many children as possible learned to read and write their mother tongue. Indeed, the attention of the missionaries was drawn to "the advantage and necessity of teaching the children to read their own language in order to their being useful to their parents and countrymen, by reading the Scriptures and religious Tracts" (Spencer 1971:537). For these reasons, the missions stepped up the production of African language materials which they believed would be useful. Such materials included Bible text translations, grammars and vocabularies. Many vocabularies/dictionaries of the late nineteenth and first half of the twentieth century are as a result of this missionary effort.

The colonial administrations were more interested in political and commercial pursuits than in educating the Africans. In fact, even when there was a growing need for skilled and moderately literate

African manpower, the colonial governments saw far enough to realize that an emerging African middle class of clerks, teachers, craftsmen and entrepreneurs had to be 'controlled' for political and economic reasons.

This attitude notwithstanding, the colonial governments did not entirely abandon educational matters to the missions. They did support them by providing grants and sponsoring the production of teaching material. They published a number of dictionaries compiled by missionaries (and non-missionaries) and continued to do so in later years. Moreover, some of the colonial governments set up official committees and language bureaux from 1930 onwards. For instance, the Inter-territorial Swahili Language Committee which had been established (in Kenya) in 1932 played a considerable role in encouraging the literary and other uses of that language in East Africa. (The Institute of Kiswahili Research in Tanzania is an offshoot of the Inter-territorial Committee.) Similarly, the Literature Bureau at Zaria (established at about the same time) was later to become the Gaskiya Corporation and subsequently the Northern Nigeria Publishing Company (NNPC) responsible for the publication of Hausa textbooks and for encouraging writings in Hausa. Nowadays, the NNPC has widened its language coverage to include other languages like Fulfulde (Fula), Kanuri and Tiv. By 1950, there were ten such 'bodies' in the British colonies responsible for the production of teaching materials and for the study of the technical and linguistic problems involved in such exercises (Spencer 1971). Due to the efforts of these bodies, 91 languages were in use in schools in the British colonies at that time.

It is worth noting that in the Belgian colonies, scholars, missionaries and non-missionaries devoted considerable attention to the languages of the Congo and Zaïre and produced materials for their teaching. According to a report submitted to UNESCO in 1951, grammars and dictionaries for 21 distinct languages of Belgian-controlled territory were available and work on 34 others was well advanced. The Belgians set up a 'Commission Linguistique Africaine' in Brussels which was responsible for the choice of languages for official use in the Belgian colonies, and for solving the problems of language standardization. It is remarkable that the Belgians gave a high priority to the study of African languages, requiring officers entering their colonial administration services to learn the chosen African languages.

At this point, it is pertinent to draw attention to a major distinction between the language policies of the different colonial governments, since they determined attitudes towards the development of the African languages themselves. It was either a policy of 'linguistic identity' based on the concept of 'cultural identity' with the colonial power (an inevitable corollary of this was an almost total rejection of the African languages in official administration and education, as was the case in most French- controlled territories), or it was a policy which emphasized 'differentiation and separate development' for the different ethnic groups in Africa and therefore endeavoured to find a place for the African languages within the educational system. Furthermore, it gave limited encouragement to the use of selected languages in local administration and education at the lower level. This policy was practised by the British and Belgian colonial administrators. It is therefore not surprising that more lexicons saw the light of day in the British and Belgian colonies.

The development of modern descriptive linguistics made an impact on the quantity and quality of lexicographical works on African languages because the people involved in their production took advantage of the training facilities provided by the Summer Institute of Linguistics (a semi-religious body) and other government-supported African Language and Area Centres in the United States of America. For this reason, there has been a shift from the fragmentary polyglot wordlists or vocabularies of earlier times to comparatively superior dictionaries such as Newman's (1979) MODERN HAUSA-ENGLISH DICTIONARY and Williamson's (1972) IGBO-ENGLISH DICTIONARY (based on the Onitsha dialect), to mention just two. A significant innovation in African lexicography has been the production of specialized lexicons such as the Hausa Language Board's (1959) GLOSSARIES OF TECHNICAL TERMS IN HAUSA and Diaw's (1976) VOCABULAIRE WOLOF DE LA FAUNE AU SÉNÉGAL.

### *Limitations*

A look at the *International Bibliography of African Lexicons* by Hendrix (1982) shows over 2600 entries, covering about 350 years of lexical literature representing about 600 languages and approximately 200 dialects of African and non-African origin (p.xiv). These include bilingual and (in rare cases) monolingual vocabularies/dictionaries as well as polyglot and specialised dictionaries. A close examination of the items listed reveals that over half are described as vocabularies by their titles. If these titles are correct, less than half can be called 'dictionaries'. When compared with the multitude of languages in Africa (1,000 as cited in Welmers 1971a), this number seems utterly inadequate. Assigning one dictionary to each African language, the distribution would be such that many languages would not have any dictionaries at all. This indeed is the reality: many languages cannot boast a single dictionary, while principal languages like Hausa and Swahili have over ten each and Afrikaans and Arabic have twenty or more.

How can this state of affairs be corrected? To the simple-minded, the answer may be to produce more dictionaries, especially for languages without any, to redo the older defective vocabularies/ dictionaries, and to compile more special-purpose dictionaries. Unfortunately, the reality is more complex; in performing these tasks, one must take into account some linguistic and extra-linguistic considerations such as the representation of orthographies, the availability of manpower and other facilities, but, most importantly, the lack of financial resources.

As regards the issue of orthography, the policies of the colonial governments have had several consequences of linguistic interest. One which has a direct bearing on lexicography is that little or no attention was given to the development of the African languages. As a result, relatively few languages have acquired an orthography and become written languages, and even fewer of the languages have shown the beginnings of a written literature. Colonial government policies aside, the attitude of African experts on language problems often militates against the resolution of orthography problems. Tucker (1971) provides an interesting example: at one West African languages orthography conference, certain phonetic letters were rejected on the grounds that they were 'symbols of imperialism'. This anti-imperialist attitude may be desirable provided it is matched by a zeal to devise a set of 'non-imperialist' or 'African' phonetic letters. Unfortunately, this zeal has not been forthcoming, with the exception of the Mann-Dalby *Thesaurus* (1987, 'with an appendix on written representation') of African languages.

With regard to the problem of manpower, there are hardly any Africans who have taken up lexicography as a full-time profession.

Most pursue it only part-time and some who are listed in dictionaries may have served only as language consultants (or, to use the most common terminology, 'language informants'). Lexicographers of African languages have come mainly from Europe or North America. Related to this problem is the absence in most African countries of societies, organizations or institutions concerned with lexicography. In view of this, one would wish that African linguists gave some thought to becoming involved in African lexicography. Their involvement should not mean abandoning their present activities. Rather, there should be a commitment to contribute individually or collectively towards the development of dictionary research in Africa. For a start, I would not hesitate to propose the formation of an association for African lexicography.

The difficulty of accessibility to publication facilities constitutes another problem for lexicography in Africa. This problem is not limited to lexicographical products; it affects all genres of publications. There are very few publishing companies and they charge exorbitant fees so that individuals cannot undertake publications without some form of financial assistance from the government or other organizations. As a matter of fact, one could say that no individual in Africa has single-handedly managed to issue a dictionary publication. Until recently, most lexicographical publications have been 'Euro-centred' in the sense that they have been primarily intended for use by Europeans who wish to learn the African languages. Moreover, these publications have been supported mainly by organizations in Europe or North America, and in a few cases by the respective African governments, provided the material is intended for use by the Africans.

Last, but not least, the financial state of most African countries imposes constraints on lexicographical projects, which receive attention only if they are considered of national priority. Perhaps the following statement by Susannah Al-Hassan, the Ghanaian Deputy Minister of Education in 1964 summed up the general view of some African governments about language issues:

> It is the intention of Government to encourage the development of all our major national languages... In the meantime, I think honourable members will agree that we have enough on our plates to keep us busy for a few more years without having to worry about language. (in Whiteley 1971:553)

This statement was made 25 years ago when language issues were definitely not 'on the plates' of government policy makers, at a time when most African states had just gained independence and were therefore faced with other, more urgent problems.

Today the situation is very different, and language issues are very much on the agenda. There is a growing interest among African governments in the development of university departments of linguistics concentrating their study and research on the local African languages. In Nigeria, for instance, except for the Universities of Technology or Agriculture, all higher education establishments undertake research into some indigenous languages. Similarly, the Universities of Abidjan (Ivory Coast), Dakar (Senegal), Legon (Ghana), Yaounde (Cameroon) and the Research Institutes at Ouagadougou (Burkina Faso), Bamako (Mali) and Conakry (Guinea), to mention only a few, are in one way or another involved in work on some of the local languages of their respective countries.

That governments support the efforts of these institutions is again exemplified by a recent development in Nigeria. The full recognition of the importance of language in national integration and development is expressed in the following statement by the Minister of Education, Professor Jibril Aminu:

> All efforts at national unity will be meaningless in the long run if they were concentrated on politics alone to the exclusion of the need for a national language. (*West Africa*; May 1-7, No. 3741, 702)

The government has appointed a 24-member Panel and given it the task of developing the major languages of Nigeria. In the words of the same Minister (Professor Aminu) addressed to the Panel:

> You are to develop our current major languages to aid the national policy on education as well as Fulfulde in order to support the nomadic education programme, one of the unique cardinal social programmes of the Babangida administration. (Ibid.)

The Panel is to work in conjunction with the Nigerian Educational Research and Development Council (NERDC) to whom it is directly responsible. The NERDC is a body whose duties are to advise government on policies relating to language issues and coordinate language development and research matters. Considering the Minister's statement, the assignment may ultimately involve the issue of development of up-to-date grammars and dictionaries for at least the major languages. For this purpose, the services of grammarians and lexicographers within and outside the Panel and NERDC will be invaluable.

*Conclusion*

The history of lexicography in Africa began as a result of European activities: exploration, evangelization and colonization. The early lexicons, whether compiled by explorers, missionaries, or colonial administrators, were 'Euro-centred', produced in Europe for Europeans rather than for African users (see Paper 3 below). Even with the emergence of modern linguistics, lexicographic works have been primarily intended for scholarly interest and not for the needs of ordinary Africans. This being the case, there may be no correlation between the importance of individual languages and the extent of its dictionary coverage.

African lexicons first appeared in the form of wordlists (from a European language, e.g. English, French or German into the local language), usually in the 500-1,000 word range appended to grammatical sketches. These wordlists were generally superficial and lacking in basic morphological detail and information on suprasegmental features such as tones and vowel length. Then came the somewhat 'larger vocabularies' (to use Newman's term). The vocabularies were generally oriented from an African language in the direction of a European language and often equipped with a reverse index. More recently, the vocabularies expanded into 'small dictionaries' which provided essential morphological information.

Today, 'full dictionaries' exist, although they may still be restricted in size by comparison with those of major world languages such as English and French. In addition to providing morphological detail, these dictionaries mark the suprasegmental features (tones and vowel length) and some even provide plates illustrating items distinctive to the culture, as in the DICTIONARY OF MODERN YORUBA by R.C. Abraham (1958). While some of these dictionaries are still conceived for European users, others, like Newman/Newman's (1977) MODERN HAUSA-ENGLISH DICTIONARY, are primarily intended for practical use by native Hausa speakers and Hause language learners, and to serve as reference works for scholars.

In recent times, the focus has been on efforts by Africans themselves to create much needed technical vocabulary covering areas such as science and technology, and language and literature. These efforts have produced dictionaries such as Mahamane's (1982) LEXIQUE SCIENTIFIQUE FRANÇAIS-HAUSA or the Dar es Salaam Legal Research Centre's and the Faculty of Law's (1968) SWAHILI LEGAL DICTIONARY. Africans have also directed their attention towards the creation of monolingual dictionaries. For instance, a project to compile a monolingual Hausa dictionary has been undertaken by a team of Hausa scholars and is now awaiting publication (cf. Newman/ Newman forthcoming). It is also worth noting that a Swahili monolingual dictionary by TUKI, the KAMUSI YA KISWAHILI SANIFU, appeared in 1981.

As African states address the issue of language development, they are, in the face of economic constraints, increasingly compelled to pay more attention to the major languages. For this reason, languages such as Duala, Hausa, Igbo, Lingala, Moore, Swahili, Wolof and Yoruba have been and will continue to be developed at the expense of the minor languages, since they serve important functions in their respective countries. It is likely therefore that lexicography will have to play a significant role in the development of these major languages in addition to providing a standard orthography for the various dialects which may exist for some of the major languages.

# 3 Lexicography in Central Africa: the User Perspective, with Special Reference to Zaïre

by Masidake Busane

*Introduction*

There are a few important studies on lexicographical activities in languages of Central Africa, either by lexicographers themselves (e.g. Benson 1964, Snoxall 1965) or by linguists (e.g. Bennett 1986, Coupez 1985, Mbogho 1985, Polomé forthcoming). The experiences and methods of pioneers of Bantu lexicography are surveyed in Benson (1964) with a view to formulating suggestions for future lexicographers, drawing on his experience in the compilation of a standard Gikuyu dictionary. Bennett (1986) criticizes the inadequate presentation of grammatical information in Bantu dictionaries and shows how, with special reference to the parsing system of kiSwahili and Gikuyu, the results of modern grammatical analysis can be incorporated in the dictionary for the benefit of the prospective user.

It is this user perspective in lexicography, and the ways it has been attended to by lexicographers working on languages of Central Africa, that this paper will focus on. The summary report of the 1960 Indiana Conference on Lexicography mentions this user perspective as the first of several points on which the conferees expressed unanimity:

> Dictionaries should be designed with a special set of users in mind and for their specific needs. (Householder and Saporta 1962:279)

The purpose and the intended users of a dictionary should indeed be guiding principles in handling the materials in lexicography, following the three headings of lexicographic work that Hartmann (1983) delineates as recording, description and presentation.

Thus, preliminary research to determine the purpose of the dictionary and to define the needs of the intended users is required in planning a dictionary project. Lexicographers and dictionary editors do not always specify the intended users of their dictionaries, in the same way as they do not expose their principles and methods of work. One way of finding out for whom their dictionaries are designed and whether, and how, user needs are satisfied is to peruse the dictionaries concerned.

In this paper the stated (and unstated) aims of dictionaries of languages used in Central Africa will be uncovered by considering the socio-cultural context in which these works were produced, by looking at the prefaces and introductions written by compilers, and by studying the methods utilized in arranging their entries. The paper will end with a discussion of current needs and some suggestions for improvements.

*The Socio-cultural Background*

The first way of shedding some light on the scope and limitations of lexicography in this area is by relating its rationale to the socio-cultural context in which it evolved. As Dubois (1981:248) puts it:

> Dictionaries reflect the cultural universe of their users at particular moments in time, and can be categorized according to the reference needs of socio-cultural groups whose parameters the lexicographer has previously identified.

Lexicographical activities were initiated in Africa in general during the colonial period as a pragmatic response to the communicative needs of the Europeans involved in evangelization, trade and administration. Dictionaries were compiled by missionaries and a few colonial administrators for the practical use of their fellow foreigners (see Paper 2 above). These works have the African language as a target language in the sense of the language to be learned by the foreigners involved in missionary, administrative and commercial activities with local people. As a consequence, these dictionaries are less informative for the African language speakers than their European counterparts whose language is predominantly used to define and describe the target language. It is therefore not surprising that these works are nowadays criticized for not serving the needs of the African user. The inability to meet the needs of the African user and the shortcomings that we notice today in these dictionaries are probably the result of the objectives pursued by the authors themselves. As Mkude (1986:35) notes about the situation of kiSwahili in contact with English, Europeans were quick to grasp the importance of kiSwahili and its usefulness for their objectives. They therefore embarked on an extensive and fairly systematic description of it. Famous names associated with these endeavours include early kiSwahili lexicographers: Krapf (a

German), Steere (a Briton) and Sacleux (a Frenchman). Their manuals were chiefly meant for the benefit of their fellow foreigners.

The financial rewards that the compilations of vocabularies and phrase books brought to their writers and their missions also indicate the context in which they were produced. In the Belgian Congo, for example, the colonial administration encouraged missionaries to engage in linguistic, ethnolinguistic and sociological studies by promising to award a special fund to the best studies published (De Jonghe 1933:17). English-speaking Protestant missionaries were actively involved in these activities in Zaïre. Thus, in a petition letter addressed by the Conseil Protestant du Congo in November 1932 to the minister of colonies, the "Conseil" draws the attention of the government to the fact that the latter had not kept its promise regarding this arrangement and had applied a policy of double standards by favouring the Roman Catholic Missions, thus contravening its own regulations as stipulated in the following terms:

> La colonie versera à la mission une somme de 3,000 FR (majorée de 75 p.c., soit 5,250 FR) pour chaque dialecte inconnu dont la mission fournira, en manuscrit, la grammaire, le vocabulaire, un croquis indiquant l'aire de diffusion et un recueil de phrases usuelles avec traduction en langue nationale. (Archives du Conseil Protestant du Congo)

Therefore, placing these works in their socio-cultural and historical context of production can enable the researcher to understand why we could not expect them to be geared to the needs of the indigenous populations.

In addition, a limited number of copies of dictionaries at this time were published in Europe (or locally in rare cases) and therefore sold at a price obviously prohibitive to African buyers. This situation has not yet changed, unfortunately, as most dictionaries of African languages are still published abroad and thus have to be imported at high cost.

### *Analysing the Prefatory Matter*

The second source of enlightenment on the intended uses of dictionaries of languages in Central Africa is the prefaces and introductions provided by the lexicographers themselves. By scrutinizing these pages, the researcher can obtain information about the audience at whom the writer aimed his/her work. Haugen (1985) who used this method to find out the goals envisaged by Scandinavian lexicographers points out that by reading numerous introductions to dictionaries one can learn what the purposes were that animated lexicographers to undertake their often tedious and always underpaid tasks. A few examples will serve to illustrate this point. For example, the title page of Van Geel's LE PLUS ANCIEN DICTIONNAIRE BANTU (1651-52) unequivocally indicates that the work was intended for his fellow missionaries:

> Vocabularium Latinum, Hispanicum, et Congense. Ad Usum Missionariorû transmittendorû ad Regni Congi Missiones
> (Latin, Spanish and Congolese Vocabulary for the use of missionaries destined to the missions of the Kongo Kingdom).

In the introduction to his DICTIONARY OF THE TSHILUBA LANGUAGE (1939), Morrison writes:

> This work is not being published for natives but is intended for the use of missionaries and other Europeans. (p.ii)

The publication of the DICTIONARY OF THE LOMONGO LANGUAGE (1928) by Mr. and Mrs. Ruskin was greatly acclaimed by their fellow Europeans, as attested in the following lines:

> This work far surpasses anything attempted before in Lomongo. Mr. and Mrs. Ruskin greatly deserve the thanks and appreciation of scores of missionaries. Besides protestant missionaries, some of the missionaries of the Catholic missions and also traders and state officials may find helpful approaches to the language of the Equator district. (*Congo Mission News* 1929, 65, p.5)

The compilers themselves make it clear that:

> This dictionary is published that the missionaries working in the Lomongo area may acquire such a knowledge of the language that they be able to preach the Gospel of the Lord Jesus Christ, and teach the natives those eternal verities which can only be known by means of a suitable vehicle of thought. (p.v)

In these two dictionaries the vocabulary of scriptural terms is thus well represented and numerous translations of biblical citations are provided in order to guide the prospective users in their evangelization tasks.

The attempts to render the foreign terms, either from dictionaries of European languages on which these links were based or from the Bible, into the African languages point to an unstated aim of the pioneers' works: they assumed the responsibilities of codifying and legislating on the languages spoken in their areas of work for their own benefit. At a time when new ideas and concepts, as well as foreign goods introduced through commerce and industry, had to be rendered intelligibly, they thought it fell to them to capture these new realities and experiences of a different life and suggest ways of expressing them in local languages. It would be interesting to explore whether dictionary makers of this period followed any consistent principles in their ways of dealing with foreign terms. In the GRAMMAR AND DICTIONARY OF THE BOBANGI LANGUAGE (1899), John Whitehead describes the method he followed to tackle this problem, in the following words:

> I was requested, on leaving Congo, to incorporate in the dictionary words to represent useful articles in the home and workshop, for which the natives had no names, the articles being of very recent introduction, and largely limited to the area of a European station. The method decided upon for obtaining these words was as follows: derive if possible from the Kisi-Kongo, and failing this, from the French, and if great difficulty arose in transliterating French terms, take the terms in English if they offer easier aspects. (p.vii)

One conspicuous example of an attempt to codify and legislate on a Bantu language is John Whitehead's other work, the MANUEL DE KINGWANA (1928) which aimed at standardizing the variety of kiSwahili called Kingwana. Whitehead's manual was produced following the realization that, while Zaïre kiSwahili is a dialect of the Zanzibar kiSwahili, it nevertheless retains a distinctive local flavour. It has enriched itself by preserving certain forms now considered obsolete in East Africa and adopted a somewhat different vocabulary over a wide area in Zaïre by additions from Bantu vernaculars and from French. It is this distinction between Kingwana and East Coast kiSwahili that Whitehead sought to establish in this book which contains in parallel texts the grammar and vocabulary of Kingwana with glosses in English and French. Protestant missionary societies, of which Whitehead was a member, aimed at unifying the different dialects of Zaïre kiSwahili for preaching purposes. Their efforts actually culminated in the publication of *La Bible en Swahili-Congo* (1960).

These efforts to standardize Zaïre kiSwahili were at odds with the determination of the Roman Catholic missionaries to discourage its spread throughout the Congo in order to promote the use of a variety of kiSwahili closer to East Coast kiSwahili. For instance, Eynde, in the introduction to his GRAMMAIRE SWAHILI SUIVIE D'UN VOCABULAIRE (1944), clearly intended for his fellow Europeans, expresses his opposition to the expansion of Kingwana and defends the use of East Coast kiSwahili instead. The objectives and the intended users of his publication can be uncovered in the following lines from that introduction:

> Ce Kingwana n'est qu'un vil baragouin, ne tenant nullement compte de règles essentielles d'accord de la vraie langue Swahili... Nous devons vous dresser contre la tendance à répandre ce 'sabir' dans notre colonie, et c'est pourquoi nous vous permettons de faire un appel à tous nos compatriotes, désireux de faire carrière coloniale, de se mettre à l'étude du vrai et pur Swahili... C'est pour les y aider que nous n'avons pas hésité à faire paraître cette nouvelle grammaire, suivie d'un vocabulaire. (p.6)

As a consequence of this situation of conflict, a dictionary which realistically accounts for the particularities of the variety of kiSwahili spoken in Zaïre has not yet been produced. Thus, the basic process of codification in the model of language planning posited by Haugen has not yet been achieved as far as Zaïre kiSwahili is concerned. This normally calls on the expertise of learned or self-taught men or women who are capable of preparing a grammar and a dictionary, usually in that order (Haugen 1985:572).

Lenselaer's DICTIONNAIRE SWAHILI-FRANÇAIS (1983) based on Johnson's STANDARD SWAHILI-ENGLISH DICTIONARY (1939)and following the steps of Sacleux's DICTIONNAIRE SWAHILI-FRANÇAIS (1939) has gone further towards recording in a major lexicographic work the variants of Swahili specific to some areas of Zaïre. In presenting this dictionary, Lenselaer touches upon the intricate problem concerning the lack of unanimity about what constitutes standard

Zaïre kiSwahili or Kingwana. He quotes the Maniema people's saying that "Kiswahili ni nyama ya tembo: kila mtu anachumia pake" which means that kiSwahili is or resembles elephant meat: each person picks up his/her own piece at the place of his/her choice. Lenselaer's objective in including some Kingwana words next to their East Coast kiSwahili counterparts is for comparative purposes only and not for the sake of promoting Kingwana as such:

> Il n'est donc pas dans les intentions de l'auteur de mettre le Kingwana en vedette, mais de le distinguer du Swahili standard. (p.11)

The lack of a systematic lexicographic treatment of this important variety of kiSwahili is most regrettable at a time when the early amateurish and often single-handed attempts at compiling dictionaries of African languages have given way to rigorous and scientifically well-documented works. Linguists specializing in African languages have noticed the shortcomings of the works done by their predecessors and a new generation of Africanists have embarked on correcting and expanding previous works, particularly on major national and regional languages. In many cases, new dictionaries have been compiled altogether which take into account the results obtained in recent linguistic investigations about tone, word-formation, language varieties, etc.

*The Arrangement of Lexical Entries*

The passages selected to illustrate earlier lexicographers' goals in the preceding section might give the reader an impression that dictionaries published later on have adopted a different perspective. On the contrary, dictionaries published in the post-independence era are still perpetuating the objectives laid down by the pioneers of lexicography in central Africa, namely to facilitate the comprehension and learning of local languages by foreigners. This goal is, of course, not always explicitly stated. But, as we shall see below, the statements made in the introductions are very often corroborated by the presentation of the material in the body of the dictionary. For instance, in the introduction to Fraas' NANDE-ENGLISH AND ENGLISH-NANDE DICTIONARY (1961) we can read:

> In this dictionary are found bits of descriptions of customs, some idioms, proverbs, sayings, some dialectal differences and colloquialisms and a little of the beliefs, which should help not only to clarify the meanings of the words under which they are described, but also to give glimpses of various facets of the social structure of the people. (p.i)

Thus, the descriptions in English of various cultural traits of the Nande people which are found in this dictionary can only benefit the English-speaking users who can easily interpret, for example, the relevance of alluding to Charlie McCarthy in the explanation of the Nande word *abo* (in Fig. 1.)

abo, eki, eky, instrument used in witchcraft, small bone or instrument in mouth or hole, when treating an ill person, to make it sound like another's voice, probably a spirit's, as a ventriloquist, as Charlie McCarthy; ebyabo, the thing which causes the illness which the witch doctor "takes out" of the person, luava amarogo, or ebyabo

Fig. 1: Extract from NANDE-ENGLISH AND ENGLISH-NANDE DICTIONARY (1961)

On the other hand, Rechenbach's objective in the SWAHILI-ENGLISH DICTIONARY (1968) is clearly specified in the introduction where it is stated that "the volume is primarily and specifically a word source for readers and translators." (p.v) The use of English to discriminate meanings and to indicate contexts of usage clearly corroborates this objective, as only English-speaking users can successfully access the information provided in the text.

Moreover, a comparison of two entries (Figs. 2 and 3) from two dictionaries of two related languages, Bobangi and Lingala, published almost a century apart, indicates that very little improvement has been achieved as far as the user perspective is concerned. Very little help is provided in these two entries for the Bobangi or the Lingala speaker who would seek help from these dictionaries to express in English or in French an idea that he/she has formed in his/her first language:

**Liböta**, *n.*, brood, child-bearing, offspring, generation, issue, litter of young creatures, seed, family; *colq.*, affability, motherliness, leniency.

Fig. 2: Extract from GRAMMAR AND DICTIONARY OF THE BOBANGI LANGUAGE (1899)

**libótá** ma- n (<-bóta): foyer; famille; filiation, généalogie; *na – lia bisó tokoyókana maldmu*: dans notre famille il y a entente parfaite; *Yézu Kristu abótámákd na – lia Davidi*: Jésus-Christ est de la descendance de David.

Fig. 3: Extract from MALOBA MA LOKOTA LINGALA/ DICTIONNAIRE LINGALA (Lingála-Français/Français-Lingála) (1985)

It is thus clear that the bulk of dictionaries of major national or regional languages referred to above still leave the African user in the lurch, because of the nature of their presentation and the arrangement of the entries. Most of these works are monodirectional and contain a wealth of information (phonological, morphological, semantic and even ethnological) about the African language that is basically intended for the sophisticated learner or the linguist interested in furthering his/her investigations about the language concerned. As a matter of fact, a preliminary knowledge of the grammar of the language concerned is recommended. Sometimes users are required to study the grammatical sketch and to master the codes provided in the introduction before using the dictionary.

The presentation of grammatical information remains a bone of contention among various Bantuists who have tried their hand at dictionary-making in this area. Basically, the problem facing lexicographers here stems from the lexicographical treatment of two grammatical features of Bantu languages, namely the inflection of nominals and verbals by means of prefixes, and the complex and productive derivational system. Bennett (1986:3-4) offers a summary of the problem involved:

> If items are alphabetized by prefix, some sectors are overcrowded and others nearly empty, and a verb will be listed far from its nominal derivatives, however transparent these may be. In the case of nouns, singular and plural differ in prefix in most cases, the degree to which singular may be predicted given the plural and vice versa varies, but there is nowhere complete predictability.

Faced with this problem, lexicographers have either listed both the singular and the plural forms of the nouns, or the singular form only. An alternative popular approach has been to arrange the lexicon by stems, thus grouping related items together.

The concern about the difficulties likely to be encountered by the users of these materials accounts for many introductory pages usually allocated to grammatical sketches of the languages concerned without the knowledge of which it is deemed hazardous to use the dictionaries successfully. We believe, however, that these sections and other introductory explanations are not sufficient provisions for a user-friendly product. Dictionary users are known to allocate little time to the study of these prefatory matters.

Strict adherence to the arrangement of items by stems can be illustrated by the following entries (Figs. 4 and 5) from the lexicons of two related languages of Eastern Zaïre, Havu and Tembo:

```
-fum-   A. être guéri, guérir d'une malacie .
           Dér  -fumu 1,2 ; 14,6 ; -fumy- .
        B. échapper à ; se soustraire à l'emprise,
           à la surveillance de qqn . Syn  -kir- B.
           V  -fulumuk- ; -ganu:l- ; -lam- B .
        C. intr  V syn  -cunguk- .
```

Fig. 4: Extract from LEXIQUE HAVU (1985)

| | | | | |
|---|---|---|---|---|
| -fùm- | kúfumá ' | | : | kupona; kuponyoka.<br>(傷, 病気が)治る：(動物が罠から)逃げる.<br>guérir (intr.), se cicatriser (maladie, blessure);<br>s'échapper (animal attrapé au piège). |
| | múfumu (1) | báfumu (2) | : | munganga, ba-.<br>医者.<br>guérisseur. |
| | búfumu (14) | máfumu (6) | : | dawa, ma-.<br>薬.<br>remède, médicament. |
| | kúfumyá (caus.) | | : | kuponesha.<br>(傷, 病気を)治す.<br>guérir (tr.), cicatriser. |
| | kúfumúkálá (intr.) | | : | kupona muzuri.<br>(人が)病気から回復する.<br>guérir (intr.), retrouver la santé. |

Fig. 5: Extract from LEXIQUE TEMBO (1985)

The main objective of the compilers here has been to indicate the relationships (morphological and semantic) that exist between the nouns and verbs derived from the same stems. Each stem is analysed morphologically and its derivatives arranged accordingly. In the case of Havu, the use of analogical methods also enabled the compiler to provide synonyms and antonyms of related items.

As we can gather, the usefulness of this presentation to the unsophisticated user is impaired by the detailed analysis itself. In many cases the phonological representation of the items differs from their morphological analysis, thus requiring the user to be aware of the morphophonological rules applicable to each case. In the introduction to the Tembo lexicon, Kaji acknowledges this difficulty:

> Malgré l'avantage de compiler un lexique par rangement des thèmes ou radicaux, l'inconvénient surgit quand on le consulte. Comment peut-on savoir le sens du mot *múfumu* rencontré dans un texte, par exemple? Il n'y aurait pas de problèmes si l'on sait que dans cette langue il y a un verbe auquel se rapporte ce nom et que son radical est - *fùm*. Mais cela suppose déjà une connaissance profonde de cette langue. (1985:xii)

As a solution, Kaji decided to add an index in which all Tembo words appearing in the lexicon are listed alphabetically, followed by their corresponding stems. This arrangement requires the user to find the stem in the index first before checking its meaning and that of related items in the larger context of the lexicon. The same method is used in Polak-Bynon's LEXIQUE SHI-FRANÇAIS (1978) which also arranges the items by their stems, but differs in the presentation of the index, which is French-Shi, i.e. stems are given as glosses of the French words listed alphabetically in the index. These are few instances in which the compilers have indicated concern about the complexity of their work and have attempted to suggest to the prospective user ways of accessing to the information included in their lexicons.

However, the problem remains as to whether all the lexical units that are likely to be derived from the main entry or the stem should be entered in the dictionary.

The entry *azima* in the KAMUSI YA KISWAHILI SANIFU (1981) (KKS) lists *-ia* (applied suffix), *-ika* (stative), *-isha* (causative), *-wa* (passive) and *-an*a (reciprocal), thus predicting the production of *azimia*, *azimika*, *azimisha*, *azimwa* and *azimana*. No definitions are provided for these derivations. In a study on productivity and the Swahili lexicon based on four Swahili dictionaries, Shepardson (1986:79-80) argues that the above suffixes should be purged from the dictionary because all five possess the potential to combine with any stem provided that they are compatible with it. In Sacleux's dictionary, the passive is entirely omitted, probably for this reason. Shepardson concludes that the predictability of the above suffixes is recognized in the KKS to some degree in that no definitions are provided. However, the listing of "acceptable" suffixes for each and every stem in the KKS is misguided.

Whether the dictionary user - and which user - is well served by the insertion of all of the attested forms is still to be investigated. Only research into dictionary use at different levels and in different contexts will help researchers solve this problem and put forward suggestions for improvement.

*Current Requirements and Suggestions*

The user perspective in dictionary production and use in Africa cannot be enhanced without due consideration of its sociolinguistic situa tion. In Central Africa, the general linguistic situation can be briefly summarized as a multilingual/multicultural one in which the European languages (English, French and Portuguese) are superimposed on national or supra-ethnic languages on the one hand, and tribal languages on the other hand.

Pierre Alexandre (1972) and John Spencer (1988) remind us, however, how misleading the terms English-speaking or Anglophone and French-speaking or Francophone are when applied to Africa. The African complex multilingualism is sometimes obscured by the fallacious use of these French loan-words Anglophone and Francophone (cf. Faik 1975). These two phrases generate particularly dangerous illusions because the number of Africans able to express themselves effectively in these two languages does not surpass 10 percent of the total population (Alexandre 1972:81). This situation attested in the 'seventies by Alexandre has not yet changed. Writing about the position of French in Zaïre, Rubango (1986) mentions a previous investigation on school bilingualism in Zaïre which indicates that, despite its status of official language, French remains an élite language in this country since only 1 out of 25 Zaïreans can speak French and only 1 out of 130 can efficiently write in it. As a consequence, most African countries have opted for a system of multilingual education that best meets the needs and aspira tions of the majority of their populations. It is generally agreed that the medium of instruction for the first three years of primary education should be the main national language spoken in the locality of the school. The foreign language is taken on as a subject of study with the hope that it will gradually become the sole medium of instruction at the appropriate level, in reality at higher education which is reached by just a minority of young people.

Some scholars have even suggested models of multilingual education involving the mother-tongue, the languages of wider communication (or trade languages) and foreign languages (e.g. Tadadjeu 1980: model of trilingual education in Cameroon). These models require, among other things, the development of language teaching materials. Yet, dictionaries are rarely mentioned in the discussions of the materials necessary to implement such programmes. We believe, however, that it is only by introducing the use of dictionaries across the curriculum at the early stages of the educational system that we can expect learners to familarize themselves with these materials and enhance dictionary reference skills for future study work. The acquaintance with the use of dictionaries involving all the languages they are acquiring should be encouraged among learners, just as the implementation of a bilingual/multilingual education will strengthen their ability and confidence in using the languages involved in their repertoire and eradicate their linguistic insecurity.

At present, dictionary use is limited to the dictionaries containing the foreign languages taught at school. As we noted in the first section of this paper, taking kiSwahili as an example, the existence of numerous dialects within a single language poses problems of standardization and codification. The compilation of learners' dictionaries for African users of the major national and regional languages will contribute to the promotion of a standardized or unified form of the languages concerned for the purposes of education and communication at various levels in the society. Their compilers should ideally include representatives of various areas where the languages dealt with are spoken.

Zaïre may be said to be located at the cross-roads of many important Central African languages. The external boundaries arbitrarily imposed during the colonial period have created a situation whereby major Bantu languages are spoken in Zaïre and neighbouring countries: kiKongo in the People's Republic of the Congo and Angola, Chokwe in Angola, Bemba in Zambia, Alur in Uganda and Zande in Sudan. Like kiSwahili, these languages have developed "local flavours" which may cause barriers to communication among communities using them on both sides of the border. Cooperation among lexicographers working in these languages is thus called for in order to bridge the gaps created by the separate developments that these languages are undergoing.

On another level, bilingual dictionaries should be compiled which involve not only the major languages of wider communication (e.g. kiSwahili-kiKongo and kiKongo-kiSwahili) but also the latter with the languages of the many ethnic groups for whom the lingua francas are only second languages (e.g. kiSwahili-Tembo and Tembo-kiSwahili).

Finally, with the increasing spread of English in Central Africa, it appears that French will have to compete not only with the African languages but also with English. As a result, we suggest that school trilingual dictionaries of English, French and African languages be compiled to cater for the needs of those being educated in this emerging linguistic situation. The availability of larger and more accurate dictionaries of major African languages, the very languages used as media of instruction, will facilitate the task of planners as these dictionaries can easily serve as sources of information for the compilation of pedagogically graded and adapted materials. This work should be done in close collaboration with the producers of the large dictionaries.

It is also hoped that the LEXIQUES THEMATIQUES DE L'AFRIQUE CENTRALE (LETAC), technical glossaries being published by the French Agence de Coopération Culturelle et Technique (ACCT) and the Centre de Recherche et de Documentation sur les Traditions Orales et la Littérature en Afrique (CERDOTOLA) will also constitute a major source for technical terms.

So far, lexicons dealing with the economic terms of kinyaRwanda, Basaa, ciLuba, kiSwahili and Monokutuba (kiKongo) have been published, while researchers in the Central African Republic have already compiled two volumes on Sango, each covering economics and education.

As far as the foreign languages are concerned, research into the development of appropriate learners' dictionaries for African users is called for.

A set reading passage is often the starting-point for vocabulary learning and an opportunity to turn to one's dictionary for help. I found the word *bride-price* in a reading passage on 'Hausa marriage' in *English-Africa*, an English course for secondary schools in French-speaking Africa developed by Macmillan (1986:75). Here follow the staggering results of an investigation into how this word, and some other words in the text describing the circumstances leading to the ceremony of African marriage, are treated in the dictionaries within my reach:

The four EFL learners' dictionaries (OXFORD ADVANCED LEARNERS' DICTIONARY, LONGMAN DICTIONARY OF CONTEMPORARY ENGLISH, CHAMBERS UNIVERSAL LEARNERS' DICTIONARY and COLLINS COBUILD ENGLISH LANGUAGE DICTIONARY) do not enter this word.

The COLLINS DICTIONARY OF THE ENGLISH LANGUAGE defines *bride-price* (or *wealth*) as "(in some societies) money, property, or services given by a bridegroom to the kinsmen of his bride in order to establish his rights over the woman".

None of the bilingual dictionaries in my possession (English-French, English-Swahili) has it.

The word that is most commonly used is *dowry*. This word is entered in my dictionaries, but has a different meaning from that of *bride-price*, viz. "the property brought by a woman to her husband at marriage" (COLLINS). The equivalents of *dowry* in Swahili and French do not offer much help either. Abstracts from some dictionaries within my reach dealing with this concept are given in Fig. 6 below.

> COLLINS-ROBERT SCHOOL FRENCH-ENGLISH AND ENGLISH-FRENCH DICTIONARY (Atkins et al. 1983):
>
> *dowry* = dot;
>
> DICTIONNAIRE DU FRANÇAIS CONTEMPORAIN (Dubois et al. 1971):
>
> *dot* = argent ou biens qu'une femme apporte en se mariant;
>
> CONCISE ENGLISH-SWAHILI DICTIONARY (Snoxall 1961):
>
> *dowry* = mahari;
>
> KKS (TUKI 1981):
>
> *mahari* = mali au fedha inayotolewa na mwanamume kupewa mwanamke au wazazi wa mwanamke anayetaka kumuoa.
>
> DICTIONNAIRE SWAHILI-FRANÇAIS (Lenselaer 1983):
>
> *mahari* = dot, biens dotaux, accord (payement) au sujet de la dot.
>
> ...
>
> (*Kgw*. mali est us. à la place de mahari).
>
> *mali* = n. biens, possessions, avoir, richesses.
>
> *Kgw*: mali est us. à la place de mahari, dot.
>
> DICTIONNAIRE DE LA LANGUE SWAHILI (Kajiga 1975):
>
> *dot* = mali ya ndoa, vitu vyenyi kuletwa na bibi ao na bwana wakati anaunga ndoa. Mahari.
>
> *mali* = bien, propriété, avoir, fortune, richesse, argent.
>
> DICTIONNAIRE DES ETUDIANTS (Monot-Chopard 1969):
>
> *dot* = mali ya ndoa.
>
> *mali* = les biens, la richesse...
>
> (ya ndoa), la dot.

Fig. 6: The treatment of *dowry/dot/mahari/mali* in several dictionaries

The inconsistency in the treatment of this concept illustrates the necessity of devising dictionaries of foreign languages for African learners. Some attempts have already been made to compile dictionaries specially intended for African learners of English and French at school level. One such dictionary that seems to have come closer to treating the word *bride-price* satisfactorily is the LONGMAN PRIMARY DICTIONARY (1985). The editors claim that their dictionary is written especially for pupils in African schools. The words which are included have been selected because they are used in textbooks or are found in school syllabuses. The compilers also attest to having consulted teachers and educational experts in Africa about what information pupils need in their dictionary. As can be seen in Fig.7, this dictionary presents the word *bride-price* as a sub-entry of *bride* with the meaning that is usually associated with it in African societies:

> **bride** /braɪd/ *noun*
> a girl or woman who is going to be married, or who has just been married
> **bridal** /ˈbraɪdl/ *adjective* of a bride or wedding.
> **ˈbride price** *or* **ˈbride wealth** *noun* payment of money or cattle made to the family of a woman when she is married. **lobola** is another word for **bride price.**
> **bridesmaid** /ˈbraɪdzˌmeɪd/ *noun* a girl or woman who helps a bride at her wedding

Fig. 7:
Extract from LONGMAN PRIMARY DICTIONARY (1982)

*Conclusion*

In the previous section of this paper, I suggested that efforts to compile dictionaries aimed at African users should be made and encouraged in order to meet their specific needs and requirements. The critical analysis of the lexicographic treatment of the concept 'bride-price', familiar to most African societies, has hopefully helped to highlight the importance for lexicographers working in this area to adopt an African user perspective in their projects. In this context, it has also appeared that the prospective users' total vocabulary, in all their previously acquired languages, can help sort out the sources of difficulty - hence the usefulness of bilingual or multilingual dictionaries. As far as learning and teaching foreign languages is concerned, I agree with Meara (1983) that a lot might be gained if we began to consider the learners' total vocabulary, in all the languages he/she knows, as an integrated whole, and not just as a set of small discrete components.

# 4 Arabic Lexicography in Northern Africa, with Special Reference to Egypt

by Nawal El-Badry

## *Introduction*

This paper is concerned with lexicographic activities in the Western region of the Moslem Empire which comprises North West Africa and Moslem Spain. In addition, it deals with the most important landmarks in the history of Arabic lexicography in Egypt, with reference to bilingual dictionaries of English and Arabic in particular. The paper concludes with a cursory look at present-day lexicographic activities in some of the Arab countries in North Africa. The paper does not attempt to report on lexicographic activities connected with other languages spoken in North African countries, such as Berber, Hausa and Nubian.

## *The Origins of Arabic Lexicography*

The arrival of Islam in the 7th century A.D. changed the status of Arabic from a language whose use was limited to the needs of a group of warring desert tribes to the status of an official language of an expanding Empire. Suddenly, its use was widened to cover not only vast territories of land, but also unlimited domains of human activity and thought. Osselton's remark that dictionaries "came into being in response to very practical needs" (1983:13) proves to be particularly relevant in the case of Arabic. The very practical needs that necessitated the compilation of Arabic dictionaries were two-fold. First, there was the need to preserve the language of the revelation so that it would not become diluted and lost to the languages of the many nations that became part of the Islamic State. Second, there was a need to impart knowledge of the language of the State to its new subjects in order to provide them with access to the new religion and jurisdiction and to enhance communication with them.

In response to these pressing needs, the first full-scale Arabic monolingual dictionary, KITAB AL-ᶜAIN (literally the Book of the [letter] ᶜAin), was compiled by Al-Khalil Ibn Ahmad (718-786 A.D.) towards the end of the eighth century. The compilation of this dictionary gave rise to a very active and scholarly tradition of lexicographic writing. This tradition lasted for about a thousand years, and participants from virtually every corner of the world of Islam have contributed to it.

*Arabic Lexicography in North-west Africa*

The whole of North Africa as well as Spain had long been provinces of the Islamic Empire (Egypt since the year 640 A.D., Morocco since 683 and Spain since 711) when Arabic lexicography was flourishing in the Eastern regions of the Empire. This being the case, one would have expected to find the newly formulated practice of dictionary-making filtering through to these parts of the State. However, it was not until late in the 10th century that lexicographic works were compiled in the Western region of the Empire which traditionally meant North Africa and Spain or Al-Andalus, as it was known then. It should be noted here that no real political divisions existed between the different provinces and that, in actual fact, scholars and authors did not recognise frontiers between countries in the whole of the vast Islamic State. Most Moslem thinkers travelled extensively from one country to another, where they met with encouragement, enjoyed sponsorship from the rulers, and stayed as long as they pleased. We therefore find that most lexicographic works that appeared in the Western region of the Islamic Empire were produced in Al-Andalus, as it was the centre for all cultural activities.

The first dictionary that was produced in the Arab West was KITAB AL-BARI', edited in the 10th century by Isma'il Ibn Al-Qasim Al-Qali (893-967 A.D.). Although by the time this dictionary was compiled some progress had already been achieved in the making of Arabic dictionaries, Al-Qali chose to follow the phonetic arrangement of AL-ᶜAIN. He also adopted its anagrammatical method.

Like its sister Semitic languages, Arabic is based on a consonantal root system, which means that virtually each word of the language is reducible to an abstract consonantal root. The vast majority of these roots are triliteral, whilst some are quadriliteral or even quinquiliteral. Al-Khalil Ibn Ahmad had not followed the usual alphabetical order in the arrangement of entries in his dictionary. Instead, he had devised a new system in which consonants were arranged according to their place of articulation, beginning with the lowermost (guttural) and ending with the outermost (labial) sounds, thus starting his dictionary with the letter *ᶜAin* which gave the book its title, KITAB AL-ᶜAIN.

The term anagrammatic method means that Al-Khalil treated all the variant permutations of the consonants of a given consonantal root before treating the next root. For example, in the case of the root *'rf* (*'arafa* meaning 'to know') which comes under the letter *ᶜAin*, he treats all the possible sequences of these three consonants, in this case *'afara* 'to dust', *ra'afa* 'to bleed', *rafa'a* 'to raise', *fara'a* 'to branch', and *fa'ara* which is non-existent as a word root. The latter case he describes as *muhmal* meaning 'neglected'. By adopting this method, Al-Khalil made sure he treated all possible Arabic word roots.

This method was soon to be replaced by a more easily accessible ordering system. However, it is remarkable that Al-Qali should have disregarded any progress already achieved and instead resorted to Al-Khalil's method of arrangement.

However, the KITAB AL-BARI' had some distinctive features, such as its extensive use of fully referenced citations. Nassar (1956) mentions that 16 names were cited in the first ten pages of the dictionary, some of these several times. Besides, he mentions 23 other authorities cited in the subsequent pages. Another important feature is the great care which the author took to indicate pronunciation. Because diacritics were predominantly used to indicate vowels which are not always explicitly indicated in Arabic writing, there was always the fear that these may be misprinted or misplaced. To avoid mistakes of this nature, Al-Qali described how a word is pronounced by actually naming the diacritics that should be used.

Al-Qali provided numerous examples of usage from Arabic poetry. He also indicated the different dialects by pointing out, for example, the dialect of the people of Egypt or the people of Hijaz, and so on.

The second Arabic dictionary written in this region was an abridgement of the KITAB AL-ᶜAIN edited by Abu Bakr Al-Zubaidi (929-989 A.D.) under the title MUKHTASAR AL-ᶜAIN. This book is held in great esteem by Ibn Khaldun, the North African historian, as well as many other commentators, as the best abridgement of AL-ᶜAIN. It is also commended for its accuracy and compactness.

The third Arabic dictionary, AL-MUHKAM WA AL-MUHIT AL-AᶜZAM, was written by Ibn Sidah (1006-1066 A.D.). This was a large dictionary which was meant by its author to include all the data dispersed in other reputable dictionaries after putting right all mistakes and inaccuracies occurring in them. AL-MUHKAM was the fifth and last of the large scale dictionaries that follow Al-Khalil's method. It is considered to be fuller, more accurate and more methodical than any of its predecessors.

Another great book, namely AL-MUKHASSAS, was also written in the 11th century A.D. by Ibn Sidah. This is a comprehensive lexicon which is arranged by subject. Although a number of lexicographic compilations of this type had already been produced in Arabic, such as KITAB AL-TALKHIS by Abu Hilal Al-ᶜAskari and FIQH AL-LUGHAH by Al-Tha'alibi, Ibn Sidah's AL-MUKHASSAS represented a great step forward in the making of lexicons. It is still thought of as the best and most comprehensive of thematic lexicons in Arabic. In his introduction to the book, Ibn Sidah explains that having completed AL-MUHKAM which is arranged by word roots to help researchers find the meaning of words they may be thinking of, he wanted to compile a counterpart arranged by subject. He found this to be of more use to the "eloquent speaker, the impressive orator and the expressive poet". Ibn Sidah intended his lexicon to be as comprehensive as possible. His plan for this work was to tackle the general before the particular, and the essential before the ephemeral. The book is divided into major topics, such as "Book of Man", "Book of Instinct", "Book of Women", and so on. Each of these books is further divided into several subheadings or sections.

In 1964 the First Symposium on Education in the Arab States of the Greater Maghreb recommended that steps should be taken by Algeria, Libya, Morocco and Tunisia to compile a modern school dictionary which should be precise and easy to use. In response to this recommendation, a new dictionary with the title AL-MUᶜJAM AL-JADID LIL-TULLAB (Students' New Dictionary) was published in Tunisia after ten years' work.

This dictionary departs from the conventional arrangement by word root. Entries are arranged alphabetically under their derived forms rather than under the traditional consonantal roots. This method has not been accepted by many linguists and lexicographers, since it scatters semantically closely related derivatives of the same root over different portions of the dictionary. The dictionary incorporates a number of appendices as well as a great deal of illustrative drawings.

A second dictionary that has been produced very recently in

North Africa is AL-MU[c]JAM AL-[c]ARABI AL-'ASASI LAROUSSE (Basic Arabic Dictionary). This book is the outcome of an eight-year project undertaken by the Arab League Educational, Cultural and Scientific Organisation (ALECSO) in Tunisia. It comprises 1,300 pages containing about 25,000 entries alphabetically arranged under their consonantal roots. It also includes many Arabised words. According to the introduction, this dictionary is aimed at "all Arabic speakers, all students of Arabic, all teachers and students, all university students in language departments and departments of Arabic and Islamic studies."

The Permanent Bureau for the co-ordination of Arabisation in Rabat has been taking part actively in the lexicographic field for over a quarter of a century. It co-ordinates the efforts of the various institutions in the Arab world concerned with the creation of new technical terminology in Arabic. The Bureau also prepares and publishes terminological lists and dictionaries.

*Arabic Lexicography in Egypt*

As we move to Egypt we find that the situation there is rather different. Egypt's location at the doorstep of Arabia and the very close connections between Sinai, the Mediterranean Sea and the Red Sea made her play an active part in the cultural life of the region. In addition, as Cairo was the capital city of the Mamluke State which extended over the whole of Syria and Egypt from the 13th to the 16th centuries, many scholars and thinkers found their way to Egypt when Baghdad was captured by the Mongols in the middle of the 13th century. [c]Umar (1970) says that an active linguistic movement existed towards the end of the third century and the beginning of the fourth century of Hijra (10th-11th centuries A.D.) in Egypt in which scholars from other provinces such as Al Dinawari and Ibn Qutaibah as well as local scholars such as Kura' Al-Naml, Ibn Wallad and Al-Nahhas took part. Kura' Al-Naml (d. 922) wrote several lexicographic works the most important of which is the AL-MUNJID or AL-MUNAJJAD (cf. Ya[c]qub 1981).

A large number of lexicographic works have been produced in Egypt. Two of these are of the greatest importance in the whole history of Arabic lexicography: LISAN AL-[c]ARAB by Ibn Manzur (1232-1311) and TAJ AL-[c]ARUS by Murtada Al-Zabidi (1732-1790).

LISAN AL-ᶜARAB is an exhaustive dictionary which incorporates to a great extent the lexicographic material included in all the Arabic dictionaries preceding it. Ibn Manzur did not claim originality in his dictionary; he himself stated that he merely quoted from previous works. As he considered the Arabic language to be endangered, he aimed to write a dictionary which he metaphorically likened to Noah's Ark. With its 80,000 entries the LISAN is considered to be the best and most exhaustive dictionary of classical Arabic. Haywood (1960) says that it is comparable in size and scope to the OXFORD ENGLISH DICTIONARY. It was first printed in 1892 in 20 volumes and later reproduced in the usual alphabetical arrangement under the title LISAN AL-ᶜARAB AL-MUHIT.

Murtada Al-Zabidi's TAJ AL-ᶜARUS is another work which assumed great importance in the history of Arabic lexicography. It was intended as a commentary on and an enlargement of Al-Firuzabadi's AL-QAMUS AL-MUHIT. Containing about 120,000 entries this dictionary is the last of the large classical Arabic dictionaries. Lane in his MADD AL-QAMUS (1968), commends the TAJ for being the most complete and copious of all Arabic dictionaries.

With regard to bilingual lexicography in North Africa, it is probably safe to say that the earliest dictionaries were those produced in Egypt for Arabic and Coptic. These were mostly compiled by Coptic priests in order to translate the language of the Coptic church for the benefit of the population who had been rapidly adopting Arabic as their tongue. One example is AL-SULLAM AL KANA'ISI compiled during the 14th century by the Bishop of Samannud, a town in the Nile Delta. It lists Coptic terms from books of the four Apostles and gives their Arabic equivalents. Another is AL-SULLAM AL-KABIR by Abu Al-Barakat Ibn Kabar which comprises 30 parts written on the same lines as Ibn Sidah's AL-MUKHASSAS (cf. Nassar 1956 and ᶜUmar 1970).

Contact with the West through the Napoleonic Campaign to Egypt resulted in greater interest in bilingual lexicography. A DICTIONNAIRE DE MÉDECIN FRANÇAIS-ARABE was edited in 1870 by Mahmud Rushdi Al-Baqli and in 1928 a very comprehensive encyclopedic ENGLISH-ARABIC DICTIONARY OF MEDICINE, BIOLOGY AND ALLIED SCIENCES was edited by Mohammad Sharaf (Ghali 1971).

Elias Antun Elias was a pioneer in bilingual Arabic lexicography.

In 1913 he produced an English-Arabic dictionary with the title ELIAS' MODERN DICTIONARY: ENGLISH-ARABIC and in 1922 he published ELIAS' MODERN DICTIONARY: ARABIC-ENGLISH for the use of Arab students. In his Arabic-English dictionary he tried to combine the conventional arrangement of Arabic entries with modern methods of lexicography by inserting "most of the derivatives in small type according to their alphabetical order followed by the Arabic roots under which they would be found enclosed in plain brackets". Elias's two dictionaries have been reprinted and enlarged several times, and for many years have remained most popular among users in many Arab countries. However, they have recently been overtaken by better dictionaries produced in Lebanon.

Since the 1930's, the Arabic Language Academy in Egypt has been taking part in lexicographic activities in the region, e.g. by producing AL-MU[c]JAM AL-WASIT in 1960. AL-WASIT is a monolingual Arabic dictionary which includes borrowed and Arabised words. Although it follows the traditional system of entering roots rather than derivatives, it includes derivatives which are thought to be problematic in their alphabetical order with cross-references to their roots.

AL-MU[c]JAM AL-KABIR is a more recent dictionary project being carried out by the Arabic Language Academy in Cairo. It is intended as a comprehensive encyclopedic dictionary, comprising data from classical sources as well as new words and modern terminology. Two parts of the dictionary have been published, one in 1970 and the other in 1982. Work has so far covered only the first letter of the alphabet.

*Conclusion*

Although some of the finest works of Arabic lexicography have been produced in North Africa, this region seems to have gone through a long period when only very little, if any, lexicographic activity was apparent. A second phase of manifest interest in dictionary-making began in Egypt in the 18th century. This phase resulted in the compilation of TAJ AL-[c]ARUS as well as a number of bilingual dictionaries of Arabic with other languages, mainly English and French. The present century, however, has witnessed a spread of interest in lexicography to all the Arab countries of North Africa, at least at the institutional level and often in association with modern linguistic studies (cf. Bakalla 1983).

Initially the compilation of dictionaries in North Africa was prompted by religious zeal. Arabic monolingual dictionaries were produced in order to preserve and explain the language of Islam, while bilingual dictionaries, e.g. Coptic-Arabic, were motivated by the desire to support Christianity in the face of the new belief.

More contemporary developments in Arabic lexicography, however, have been motivated by the need for communication with Europe and the rest of the world. This has resulted in the production of numerous bilingual dictionaries, both general and technical.

# 5 The impact of computer technology, with special reference to Eastern Africa

by Michael Mann

*Introduction*

Some participants in this Workshop have recently been hearing of the new edition of the OXFORD ENGLISH DICTIONARY, with 500,000 entries occupying 20 volumes, prepared from the earlier edition, supplements and new material with the help of computers in a mere six years, at a cost of more than £7 million. The intention of this paper is more modest, to consider how an African lexicographer can benefit from the technology of the affordable personal computer.

I do not propose to say anything in any detail about the ways in which computers have been used to analyse printed texts and produce indexes of words or concordances, because there are very few texts in African languages that are already stored in computers, and it is doubtful whether lexicographers will think it worth their time to type texts for the purpose. Nevertheless, where texts are available, concordances, indexes or wordlists can be of great value to lexicographers. Figure 1 contains a short extract from a concordance of verbal forms in the first two chapters of a Swahili novel.

| | | |
|---:|---|---:|
| Nimewa**jengea** | kwa huko nyuma ya nyumba | 11.4 |
| Sajin Paolo ali**sogea** | mbele ya meza ya Spekta | 14.3 |
| bila shaka alikuwa akim**ngojea** | Spekta Seif | 13.3 |
| alisimama pale ... akim**ngojea** | Spekta Seif | 18.3 |
| kakaa kwa sababu ya kum**ngojea** | mtu ambaye anamwona kakawia | 17.1 |
| Bwana Msa, bila ya ku**ngojea** | kuambiwa, alivuta kiti | 7.4 |
| aliona wame**tokea** | kunako vijumba vya udongo | 16.3 |
| wali**tokea** | kunako uwanja mkubwa | 17.1 |
| wali**tokea** | nyumbani kwa Spekta Seif | 9.3 |
| tumebaki...hapo stesheni alipo**tokea** | huyu bwana mgeni wako | 10.7 |
| Ziraili anaanza kuni**nyembelea** | | 22.1 |
| Seif aka**endelea** | na hadithi yake | 15.4 |
| ali**endelea** | "Nimekutana na yule bibi ..." | 14.3 |

Figure 1
Edited extract from a verbal concordance of *Kisima cha Giningi* by Muhammed Said Abdulla.
Verb roots are in bold type; verbs are arranged according to their endings, because Bantu verbs are inflected with prefixes.

*Word-processing*

The most obvious but very important use of a small computer for a lexicographer is as a simple word-processor. The two dictionaries illustrated in Figures 2 and 3 were prepared in essentially this way (although since this was several years ago, the computer used was in fact a large University computer); in each case an early draft was first typed into the computer, then the dictionary was progressively revised over several years as research progressed; at any stage it was possible to print out the whole dictionary or any section of it to circulate to consultants. Finally the printed pages were prepared directly from the draft held in the computer. The computer relieves the lexicographer of all retyping, and at every stage the work is neat and easy to show to colleagues, consultants and potential publishers.

**gàdqan** (**gàdqaana**): *m* gadflies, horse-flies, clegs [*taons* mpl]; *sgt* **gadqàntu** *m*
**gadqe**: *f* obsidian, black volcanic rock [*obsidiane* f, *roche* f *volcanique noire*]; **+gadqèyta**; *pl* **gadqeeqi** *f*
**gadqèyta**: *m* flint or chip of **gadqe** [*fragment* m *du* **gadqe**]; *cf* **gadqe**
**gadbo**: *f* plate made of reeds/grass [*assiette* f *en roseau*]; *var* **gabdo**; *pl* **gàdob** (**gàdoobu**) *m*
**gàdda**: *m* wealth, riches [*richesse* f]; *syn* **gaddaliino**; **gaddaale**: *f* rich woman [*femme riche* f]; *syn* **taayirto**; **gaddaàli**: *m* rich man [*homme riche* m]; *syn* **taayìrtu**; *pl* **gaddaleela** *f*; idio. **"Gàdda gey!"** "Thank you" [*"merci"*] (<**gadda gey!** riches get!)

Figure 2
Extract from AN AFAR-ENGLISH-FRENCH DICTIONARY (Parker & Hayward 1985)

**golkipër** E *Goalkeeper.* F Gardien du but. ◊ <E.
**golmal** E 1. Untidy, messy, wrong; 2. Untidily, messily, wrongly. F 1. Désordonné, malpropre, mal; 2. Sans soin, à tort. ◊ <H *ghol-mel* "mixture, mixing', *ghâl-mel* 'jumbled' Forbes 1859, cf Anglo-Indian *goolmaul* 'a muddle, confusion' Yule & Burnell 1886:296
**gom** E Rubber (eraser). F *Gomme* (à effacer). ◊ <F.
**gom elastik** E Rubber (eraser). F *Gomme* (à effacer). ◊ ?<K.
**gom lak** E Kind of resin used by cabinet-makers prior to varnishing. F *Gomme laque.* ◊ <F.

Figure 3
Extract from DIKSYONER KREOL MORISYEN(Baker & Hookoomsing 1987)

Use of the computer has other advantages. For example, it is possible to make systematic changes in spelling or layout, or to create various kinds of indexes, including in the case of bilingual dictionaries, an index from glosses to entries. Several such possibilities will be illustrated below; some may require the assistance of a programmer for their realisation, but the task is not large, provided the lexicographer is systematic and can explain what is needed unambiguously. Alternatively, the necessary programming skills are not too difficult to learn using a modern programming language such as Icon.

In the case of the Afar dictionary (Afar is an Afroasiatic language spoken in Djibouti and Somalia), the authors originally used a spelling based on that used for Somali; at a late date they decided to change the spelling in conformity with a new standard emerging in Djibouti: within Afar words, every *p* had to be changed to *x*, every *x* to *c*, and every *c* to *q*. This was in fact done by a programmer, because of the difficulty of applying the change to Afar words only, and not to English or French; Afar words were distinguished by being typed entirely in capitals within the computer file, but other conventions could have been used, such as prefixing each source-language word with an asterisk, or, if the layout is sufficiently strict, punctuation alone may be sufficient to mark off entry-words and sub-entries from other matter. (In any case, eventually the printer will want to know what to print in what style of type, using his computer). Without the benefit of a programmer, the change in spelling could still have been made using the *global editing* facilities available with most word-processors: first change every *C* to *Q*, then every *X* to *C*, then every *P* to *X* (note the significance of the order: if we had done it in the opposite order, *P*s would first have been changed to *X*, then into *C* (along with the original *X*s), then into *Q* (along with original *X*s and *C*s)).

Another example: in a vocabulary of iciBemba (a Bantu language spoken in Zambia), no decision had been reached as to how tone was finally to be represented, so the vocabulary was initially typed with low-toned vowels in lower-case letters and high-toned vowels in upper-case, as in Figure 4a, in the knowledge that this could easily be converted by computer either into a diacritic representation (as in Figure 4b) or into an analogue representation (as in Figure 4c). (The diacritic representation can be achieved by global editing, but the analogue representation required further programming.)

(a) `ulUbolA` sting (of bee); ~ `lwAmutwE` violent headache
(b) `ulúbolá` sting (of bee); ~ `lwámutwé` violent headache
(c) `ulubola` [_¯_¯] sting (of bee); ~ `lwamutwe` [¯_¯] violent headache

Figure 4

Extract from an iciBemba vocabulary (a) as typed; (b) with diacritic representation of tones; (c) with analogue representation of tones

*Making indexes to dictionaries*

During the preparation of the Afar dictionary, indexes were made both from English glosses and French glosses referring to the Afar headwords, but these were not included in the published dictionary. They were immediately used as a tool in checking the treatment of synonyms and words of related meaning, and Dr Parker is now drawing on the material to write an English-Afar dictionary for the use of Afars.

It was noted at the Workshop that the great majority of African language dictionaries are descriptions of the African language for non-speakers, i.e. they are $L_2$ decoding dictionaries. The type of index that can be produced from such dictionaries will likewise be of most direct use to the non-speaker, this time as an encoding tool, although it can provide material for the compilation of dictionaries of European languages for African users. However, when we begin to see bilingual dictionaries that are essentially descriptive of say English, but written in an African language, similar indexes made from these will provide important encoding tools for African users.

Reasons why encoding dictionaries from language *A* to language *B* (for speakers of language *A*) differ from *A-B* decoding dictionaries (for speakers of language *B*) include divergent ranges of meaning associated with comparable words in the two languages, extending further to the use of different parts of speech to express the same idea. Figure 5 consists of a translation from English to iciBemba, followed by a translation back into English of the iciBemba version. The translation is typically longer than the original (the more so because of the differences in social culture); the iciBemba version uses proportionately far more verbs (23 against 6, italicised in the text – in the re-translation, hyphens have been used to indicate roughly what is rendered by each verb-form); on the other hand, iciBemba uses hardly any adjectives (shimoshimo "some", rendering "*certain*"; fyonse "*all*"; "*younger*" and "*retired*" are represented by choice of nouns, "lives its *own* life" is descriptively expanded, "*earliest* opportunity" is rendered "as soon as...", "*compensatory*" is represented by verbal recapitulation, and "*southern*" by a verbal phrase "where it is not cold in winter"); in fact, iciBemba only has some thirty words that can be classified as adjectives.

> In general however the younger generation *lives* its own life, *migrating* to the towns at the earliest opportunity. There *is* practically no compensatory movement of people to the village, except for certain southern areas where "*retired*" people *hope* to *eke* out their pensions and their life as peaceably as possible.
>
> Ala abalumendo naabakashaana baaino-myaka *naabaafya*. *Tabalefwaya ukwikala* mumishi *nookubombela* abakalamba utumilimo iyoo, nga caakuti *bamona* utulupiiya twabulendo *noowakuya-tandalila* mumataauni, *emiyiile*. *Noowakufumako ukwisa-ikala* mumishi *teewakumona*, kanofye muncende shimoshimo *umushitalala* pamwela, eko abakote-cisungu bamobamo *bakuukila*, *abati twalipoka* utulupiiya *twamwabombeeni*, muno-taauni *teepakwafya*, *naatuye* kulya kumushi, *ekwakushita* fyonse *tuleefwaya* pamutengo *wanaka*, *nookwikala* kuti *twaikalafye* umutende *nookupamfiwa* iyoo.
>
> So then the young men and girls of these times *are-difficult*. They *don't-want to-live* in the village and *perform* little services for their elders, not at all, so soon as they have *acquired* a little money for the journey and *someone-to-stay-with* in town, *it's-off-they-go*. As for *someone-coming-from-there to-come-and-live* in the villages, *there's-no-one-to-be-seen*, except in some places *where-it-is-not-too-cold* in winter, that's where some pretentious old men *move-house* to, *saying we've-received* our little *retirement* money, here in town *it's-not-half-difficult, let-us-go* to the village, *that-is-where-we-can-buy* everything *we-want* at an *easy* price, and *as-for-living we-can-live* there in health and peace *without-being-disturbed*.

Figure 5

Extract from a translation into iciBemba and re-translation into English; verbal forms are italicised to show the more extensive use of verbs in iciBemba

In the absence of exact verbal equivalences between languages, a lexical index used for encoding does not seek to give "equivalent" words in the target language, but rather a selection of words that it would be "useful to look up" in the decoding dictionary if one is seeking to express a particular meaning. (University students of Latin and Greek are – or were – expected to learn the languages by reading and by browsing through Latin- or Greek-English dictionaries without any recourse to English-Latin or -Greek dictionaries; lexical indexes provide a less severe régime.)

<table>
<tr><td>-paap-: ~ umwana %(give birth) to, %carry on back.</td><td>give birth, carry</td></tr>
<tr><td>~il- give birth to another child after %twins.</td><td>twins</td></tr>
<tr><td>~ikish- %lift on another's back. ~ikan- become</td><td>lift</td></tr>
<tr><td>%piled on each other (thin things); become %folded</td><td>piled, folded</td></tr>
<tr><td>several times. ~ikany- cs. im|paapo %infant in</td><td>infant</td></tr>
<tr><td>arms. |kapaapá %carrier of chief. ím|paapí</td><td>carrier</td></tr>
<tr><td>%(extra %load) on top.&bearer</td><td>extra load, load, bearer</td></tr>
<tr><td>í|paapá %shell, %husk, %skin of beans etc.</td><td>shell, husk, skin</td></tr>
<tr><td>úmu|páápa %(plank %tree). úlu|~ seed.</td><td>plank tree, tree</td></tr>
<tr><td>ici|paapaala flat wood %chip; ~ caaliinso</td><td>chip</td></tr>
<tr><td>%(bone round eye). &socket of eye, eye-socket</td><td>bone round eye, socket of eye, eye-socket</td></tr>
</table>

Figure 6
Extract from a vocabulary of iciBemba (in large type on the left), with raised characters showing the markings made to create index-entries for the glosses on the right

Figure 6 represents an early attempt to produce such a lexical index by marking the text of the original vocabulary. The index refers always to the main headword, and not to the sub-heads included within the same paragraph, and it is plain that in no sense is for instance -paap- the "equivalent" of *twins, lift, infant, load* etc. There is provision also for index-entries that do not actually occur in the text, but that are more likely to be looked up, e.g. *eye-socket* for *bone round eye*. In constructing this index, every entry was explicitly selected, usually by prefixing "%"; more recent indexes select most of the index-entries automatically, but allowing the lexicographer to intervene to modify the mechanical selection.

Thus in constructing an English index for the Afar dictionary, the program would automatically take the first word of each gloss (where several glosses were separated by commas, it would take the first of each); thus, "flint or chip of obsidian" would yield *flint*, but "flint, chip of obsidian" would yield both *flint* and *chip*. Sometimes the first word would be inappropriate, for instance "black volcanic rock" would yield *black*; in this case the lexicographer would insert % before the selected word; sometimes two or more words would be required, for instance *sleeping sickness*, or maybe qualification and noun should be inverted: *pot, cooking*. In this case _ and ~ would be used between words (though both would be converted to space in printing the dictionary): "sleeping_sickness", "cooking~pot".

The French index was completed without any intervention by the lexicographer. However, instead of blindly taking the first word of every gloss, the computer first removed from the start of the gloss those lexical formulæ that we might translate in English "act of ...", "sort of ...", "become ..." etc. Details are given in Figure 7. The result is not perfect, but the relatively few infelicities (such as *mauvaise odeur* "bad smell" under *mauvaise* "bad") can be put right with a word-processor.

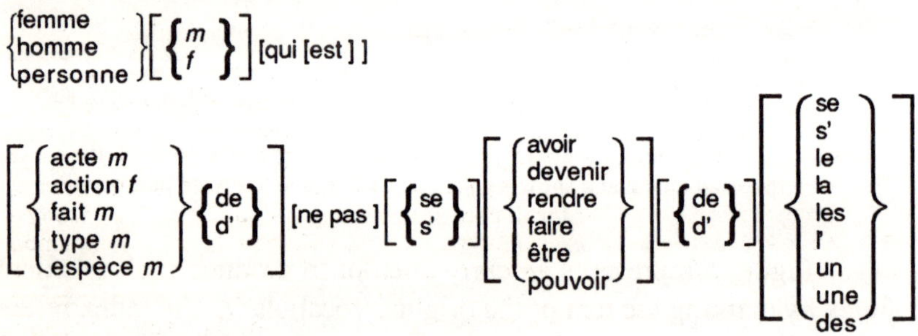


Figure 7

Formulæ omitted from the start of French glosses in constructing a French-Afar lexical index; alternative expressions are bracketed {...}, expressions that may or may not be present are bracketed [...]

Figure 8 shows another kind of index that the computer makes possible; it is a reverse index (or "rhyming" index) to the entries and sub-entries in Johnson's STANDARD SWAHILI-ENGLISH DICTIONARY. Words in this dictionary are notoriously difficult to find, partly because many words are grouped under a single main entry on a sometimes dubious etymological basis, but also because kiSwahili along with other Bantu languages has alternating noun-class prefixes. The computer allows a dictionary to be rearranged or indexed in any order; the virtues of this particular order for kiSwahili are that it enables any stem to be found easily, irrespective of the particular prefix it may be cited under in the dictionary; as word-derivation affects the end of words (in contrast to grammatical inflection which generally affects the beginning), the order facilitates the study of derivation – for instance in Figure 8 many of the verbs ending in -za are causatives; words heard in continuous kiSwahili speech are most easily found in a reverse index, since the stress falling on the penultimate syllable makes it easier to identify the end of a word than the start; and finally, as the alternative name suggests, a rhyming index may have a special interest for Swahili poets (which is most waSwahili!). Other orderings that might be useful for kiSwahili include an ordering by stem (ignoring noun-class-prefixes) and an ordering by consonants (ignoring vowels), which would bring together the many kiSwahili words borrowed from different forms of a single Arabic root.

| | | | |
|---:|---:|---:|---:|
| =puza | =zua: mzuza | kipapae | =bemba: bembe |
| =puliza: =puza | kelb: kalab | tarabe | wembembe |
| =chipua: =chipuza | sahib | bee: ebbe | chembe |
| =para: =paruza | sahib: mamsahib | debe | jembe: chembe |
| =kwaruza | =ajabu: ajib | mkebe | jembe: kiembe |
| ]=churura: | kelb | zebe | jembe |
| =churuza | chub | =shiba: shibe | jembe: kijembe |
| ziara: =zuruza | =abudu: abd | kibe | mlembe |
| =suuza: =suza | rushd | mikambe | membe |
| =tuza: tuza | seyyid | =pamba: -pambe | kinembe |
| =tuza | saidi: seyyid | =pamba: mpambe | pembe |
| =chuuza | hudhud | wambe | pembe: upembe |
| =suuza | gae | embe | |
| =uza: mwuza | gae: kigae | mwembe: embe | |

Figure 8
Extract from a reverse index to Johnson's *Standard Swahili-English Dictionary*

*Conclusion*

Of necessity, what has been said in this brief presentation is illustrative only, and must be fitted to the circumstances of different scholars by an exercise of the imagination. With the power of the computer at our disposal, lexicography becomes much less of a drudge, and the appearance of a printed volume can be not the end of a lexicographical enterprise, but a staging-point in an ever-extending and ever-branching journey.

# 6 Information Categories in Dictionaries, with Special Reference to Southern Africa

by Rufus Gouws

*Introduction*

In his discussion of reference works and technologies, McArthur (1986:19) regards dictionaries as 'containers of knowledge'. Dictionaries are compiled for specific users with specific linguistic needs, and these particular target users should determine the kind of information to be included as well as its extent. As containers of knowledge, dictionaries should accommodate a variety of information types. However, the main emphasis has to be on the function of the dictionary as a linguistic instrument and therefore the information should primarily be aimed at the linguistic needs of the target users.

Although the inclusion of a certain amount of non-linguistic information in dictionaries can be justified within the scope of its role as 'container of knowledge', this paper will not refer to the non-linguistic information types, but will only focus on aspects concerned with the linguistic character of dictionaries.

*South Africa's Multilingual Nature*

South Africa is a multilingual country. Besides a number of languages with very limited speakers' communities and a variety of European and other non-African languages being used, a total of eleven language groups can be identified. Along with Afrikaans and English, nine indigenous African languages are spoken in South Africa: seTswana, siXhosa, siZulu, siSwati, South-Ndebele, North-seSotho, South-seSotho, Tsonga and Venda. Of these indigenous languages, siZulu, siXhosa, seSotho and seTswana have the largest speakers' communities.

In spite of this variety of languages, South Africa only has two official languages, i.e., Afrikaans and English. This can be motivated demographically. Afrikaans and English are the only two languages without regional or ethnic restrictions. They are spoken throughout the country by members of all the different population groups. In contrast to this national character of Afrikaans and English, all the indigenous languages are only used on a regional basis. The historical and political background to this situation will not be discussed in this paper.

South Africa's multilingual nature demands a lexicographical policy aimed at the specific needs and problems of the different language groups. This should be part of a more comprehensive language planning policy by which the co-existence and interaction of the various languages are determined. Unfortunately, no such language planning or lexicographical policies exist. The absence of such a policy is detrimental to lexicographical practice. An analysis of the dictionary types available in the various languages indicates a complete lack of lexicographical planning. It could, for instance, be expected that learners' dictionaries should feature in the lexicographical work done on every language spoken in South Africa. The language contact situation in South Africa demands pedagogical dictionaries in order to ensure communicative success. This need has not been met. Afrikaans, for example, has no learners' dictionaries, and intensive research still has to be done to determine the lexicographical needs of the users of the various indigenous African languages.

At present, an attempt is being made, however, to rectify the situation, and a comprehensive project is underway to provide a series of translation dictionaries aimed at the needs of the different learner groups. The problem is also addressed on an academic level, in Alberts & Mtintsilana (1988) and Otto (forthcoming). The uneven availability of dictionary types needs an analysis and discussion of its own which will not be attempted in this paper.

*Uneven Coverage of Information in Dictionaries*

A comparison of dictionaries as well as the analysis of a single dictionary inevitably provides proof of the uneven coverage of various information categories. Regarding the lexicographical work done in South Africa, a distinction can be made between two types of uneven information coverage. On the one hand, it can be shown that dictionaries for the different language groups do not exhibit a similar degree of lexicographical sophistication and variety. On the other hand, the dictionaries of one specific language group do not treat all information categories alike, and within one dictionary an unbalanced presentation of information categories can often be identified.

This paper offers an account of this distinction as well as a brief discussion of the two types. Having discussed this distinction, an attempt is made to establish the cause of the uneven treatment. It is argued that this uneven coverage of information in different dictionary types as well as in dictionaries for different language groups can primarily be attributed to the lack of a sound linguistic base. Although reference will be made to dictionaries of various languages, supplemented by a more detailed discussion of some of these aspects, the main emphasis of this paper will be on Afrikaans dictionaries.

An account of the history of Afrikaans lexicography (cf. Gouws 1986, 1989, forthcoming; Heestermans forthcoming) indicates a clear evidence of a shift in lexicographical goals. The early Afrikaans dictionaries were predominantly intended for non-linguistic purposes, for example, the improvement of cultural and socio-political relations. These dictionaries were also dominated by a definite utility principle. The development of Afrikaans lexicography led to an enhancement of the linguistic character of dictionaries because a shift in emphasis provided the lexicographer with a set of linguistic goals. Lexicographers soon realized that a dictionary has to be employed as an efficient linguistic instrument.

The lexicographical goals of the majority of English dictionaries in South Africa coincide with those of British and, to a lesser extent, American English dictionaries. Due to the status of English as one of the official languages and the fact that South African English originates from the British colonial era and therefore does not differ much from British English, the English dictionaries used in South Africa are mostly British products and will not be dealt with in this paper. Monolingual English dictionaries produced in South Africa include various school dictionaries and the DICTIONARY OF SOUTH AFRICAN ENGLISH. The DICTIONARY OF SOUTH AFRICAN ENGLISH is targeted at regionalisms in South African English and the most obvious deviations from standard British English. Although dealing with a restricted subset of the lexicon, it offers a comprehensive amount of information. Its treatment of pronunciation can be regarded as one of the best attempts in this regard in South African lexicography.

Being used as official language, with English as its stable-companion, has been advantageous to Afrikaans in many ways. One of the positive results of this situation has been the attempt to provide dictionaries that can equal the standard of the English dictionaries being used. Unfortunately, the same impetus has not affected the lexicographical activities regarding the different indigenous languages. These dictionaries have had to negotiate different lexicographical goals, and the lack of linguistic competition with English has been detrimental to their lexicographical progress.

A lot of work has been done to promote lexicographical activities on the various indigenous African languages. This has resulted in a wide range of dictionaries. Unfortunately, the majority of these dictionaries are the products of limited efforts not reflecting a high standard of lexicographical achievement. These dictionaries are primarily governed by utility rather than linguistic principles, and only a limited set of linguistic information categories are accounted for.

The dominant utility principle is the attempt to improve communicative competence by accommodating these languages with Afrikaans and/or English in so-called translation dictionaries. Alberts and Mtintsilana (1988) indicate that there are almost 100 translation dictionaries involving Afrikaans and the various indigenous languages. Unfortunately, the scope. comprehensiveness and quality of information coverage do not match the quantity of dictionaries available. With a few exceptions, these dictionaries offer only restricted translation equivalents, aimed at decoding, with no or little attention given to the encoding function of a pedagogical dictionary.

By restricting the linguistic scope of the dictionary, the lexicographer also restricts its value as a linguistic tool, because there is less information to be exploited by the user. This results in a vicious circle, with the dictionary user not realizing what he can expect to find in his dictionary or how to interpret the given entries because the lexicographer does not include all the possible information categories or treat them on an equal basis. Dictionary users are often criticized for not utilizing their dictionaries or not displaying enough lexicographical skills. However, lexicographers have the responsibility to compile their dictionaries in such a way that the user can understand and utilize them as comprehensive sources of linguistic information.

The indigenous African languages display a lack of comprehensive monolingual lexicographical description. Important aspects of linguistic information like semantics, syntax and pragmatics are neglected because the scope of translation dictionaries only allows a restricted treatment of these categories.

Because Afrikaans is used on a national basis, unimpeded by

regional restrictions and has a sizeable speech community, there is a growing demand for a variety of dictionary types. Afrikaans lexicographical endeavours have resulted in an extensive collection of dictionaries, ranging from the comprehensive WOORDEBOEK VAN DIE AFRIKAANSE TAAL, various desk and smaller descriptive dictionaries to a variety of translation dictionaries and numerous special-purpose dictionaries. Reflecting the full social reality of language and its use, Afrikaans dictionaries can be regarded as functional containers of linguistic information, even though they are open to critical analysis.

The uneven coverage of information will be illustrated here by a brief account of three different linguistic categories that are included in Afrikaans dictionaries: (a) semantic, (b) normative, and (c) lexicological information. It will be shown how dictionaries give preferential treatment to semantic information. With regard to normative information it is argued that too narrow a scope is allocated to normative aspects. In reflecting on lexicographical information, the macrostructural choice displays a definite word bias whereas the macrostructural treatment of other lexical elements is neglected.

*Semantic Information*

Different subdomains of linguistics should be reflected in a dictionary article, ensuring a comprehensive information transfer to guarantee the user access to the most important properties of a specific lexical item. These linguistic properties include, amongst, others semantics, syntax, morphology, phonology and etymology. Although Afrikaans dictionaries include most of these categories, they are not treated on an equal basis, and a definite semantic bias is displayed. (This bias is not unique to Afrikaans dictionaries, but also occurs frequently in other languages; see for example Hausmann 1981:73).

The semantic bias is evident in both monolingual and translation dictionaries. It can be argued convincingly that semantic information should be regarded as the category most commonly looked up in a dictionary (cf. Al-Kasimi 1977:36). The lexicographer should not allow this fact to have a detrimental influence on the extent and nature of other linguistic information types that should be accounted for at the microstructural level. The lexicographer will do well to treat all the entries with equal care.

Within the wider field of semantics, the lexicographer is primarily concerned with lexical semantics because this is the subdomain directed at the meaning attached to lexical items. But there is more to lexical semantics than a mere description of the meaning of a lexical item, and the lexicographers of general monolingual and translation dictionaries have three main assignments regarding the inclusion of this information in the dictionary. The three aspects to be considered are: (a) the description of lexical meaning, (b) the presentation of translation equivalents, and (c) the indication of semantic relations.

Granted that the need for meaning description and translation equivalents is stronger than that for semantic relations, a distinction should be made between 'primary' and 'secondary' semantic information, with meaning description and translation equivalence the primary semantic information category and semantic relations the secondary category. This secondary category should be regarded as typical of dictionaries that give an account of advanced lexicographical achievement. It also presupposes a more comprehensive linguistic function of the dictionary.

This paper does not discuss the lexicographical treatment of semantic relations in any detail. An attempt is only made to indicate the different types and to show that they are neglected in dictionary articles.

The presentation of semantic relations can be either implicit or explicit. The lexicographer should consider the insertion of three different types of semantic relations: (a) semantic inclusion, (b) semantic opposition, and (c) semantic linking. Semantic 'inclusion' refers to an indication of hyponomy and synonymy; semantic 'opposition' has relations like antonymy, complementarity and converseness in its scope, whereas semantic 'linking' focusses on the relations holding between lexical items that are ungradable points on a scale.

Semantic linking can be explained by words like *idiot*, *imbecile* and *moron*. These words refer to different degrees of retardation, but the relation between them cannot be explicated by gradable qualifications. An imbecile is closer to an idiot on the scale of retardation than a moron. However, an imbecile cannot be described as 'more idiotic', whereas a moron is 'less idiotic'. These words share a common denominator, i.e. their reference to a form of 'retardation', and this reference constitutes the semantic link between them. This link should be indicated in the dictionary by including cross-references to lemmas that constitute other points on the same semantic scale. The lemmas *idiot*, *imbecile* and *moron* could be defined as follows:

> *idiot* "Person with a IQ below 25; see *imbecile*, *moron*."
> *imbecile* "Person with an IQ between 25 and 50; see *idiot*, *moron*."
> *moron* "Person with an IQ between 50 and 70; see *idiot*, *imbecile*."

This kind of information transfer not only gives a description of the meaning of the lemma, but also conveys information regarding the relationship of the lemma to other items in the same semantic field by including a reference that explicates the semantic link.

This information type is still neglected to a very large extent in Afrikaans dictionaries. Of the different semantic relations, semantic inclusion is treated most comprehensively, especially as far as synonymy is concerned. Hyponymy is normally given by an implicit transfer of information. Reference to this way of dealing with semantic information should be made in the front matter of a dictionary.

Unfortunately this is not normally done in Afrikaans dictionaries. The indication of semantic opposition does not have to allow for a detailed presentation of all the different types of oppositeness. The lexicographer could use a generic label like OPP. to mark the microstructural elements that constitute semantic opposites of a lemma. Although Afrikaans dictionaries make provision for this type of entry, it is done on a very limited scale. Even more exceptional is the indication of semantic links.

Judged from a linguistic point of view, Afrikaans-English translation dictionaries can be regarded as the most sophisticated bilingual dictionaries available in South Africa. This can be attributed to the fact that Afrikaans and English are the two official languages of South Africa. Because the typical user of these dictionaries has a fairly good command of both the source and the target language, lexicographers can raise the standard of their work by including, for example, a more extensive vocabulary. Although the listing of translation equivalents and the primary semantic information in translation dictionaries is usually adequate, these dictionaries often lack a sound treatment of secondary semantic information.

Translation equivalents in Afrikaans-English dictionaries can mislead the dictionary user in two ways. Firstly, homonymous words are sometimes listed as polysemous entries. In the GROOT

WOORDEBOEK/MAJOR DICTIONARY only a single lemma *cosy* is included. The following Afrikaans equivalents are given:

> "teemus; hoekbankie;... gesellig; behaaglik, knus."

According to the typographical conventions of the GROOT WOORDEBOEK, the translation equivalents of multiple senses of a lemma are divided by semicolons. Where there is a synonymous relation between two or more equivalents, these synonyms are divided by commas. The listing of the translation equivalents of the lemma *cosy* implies that *teemus* (covering put over a teapot), *hoekbankie* (corner seat), *gesellig* (pleasant and friendly), and *behaaglik, knus* (warm and comfortable) represent multiple senses of the lemma. Polysemy only applies to *gesellig* and *behaaglik, knus*, with *teemus* and *hoekbankie*, representing translation equivalents for two other homonymous lexical items *cosy*. The distinction between homonymy and polysemy is not dealt with satisfactorily in translation dictionaries.

Secondly, the dictionary user is misled by an insufficient distinction between translation equivalents representing different polysemous senses of a lemma and translation equivalents that are target language synonyms. Unfortunately, lexicographers do not strictly adhere to the above-mentioned typographical distinction between these two types of translation equivalents. Too often words are listed as synonyms instead of translation equivalents of different polysemous senses of the lemma. In the GROOT WOORDEBOEK the Afrikaans lemma *lastig* has the following translation equivalents:

> "troublesome, burdensome, annoying, forward, fractious, bothersome, importunate, pestilent; petulant; knotty, awkward ...; difficult, delicate (matter); cumbersome; cumbrous; ..."

The lemma *lastig* is a polysemous lexical item with *importunate*, *forward* and *fractious* as three of its senses. However, these three words are not synonyms, as the GROOT WOORDEBOEK indicates. Regarding secondary semantic information, a distinction should be made between absolute and partial synonyms. Afrikaans-English translation dictionaries fail to convey this information.

*The Normative Approach*

It has become a convention among lexicographers to be descriptive rather than prescriptive. However, for the average user the dictionary remains an authoritative source of information which is still regarded as a prescriptive instrument. According to Hartmann (1983:116), dictionaries and their compilers play an important role in the standardization of language. This prescriptive responsibility of the lexicographer should urge him to include more information in his dictionary articles. Because Afrikaans is a relatively young language, dictionaries still play a major role in the standardisation process. Afrikaans dictionaries are often consulted to ascertain the correct spelling or pronunciation of a lemma, the plural or diminutive form of a noun, or to enquire whether a specific form receives lexicographical approval and recognition. The dictionary user needs an indication of correctness, and he puts his trust in the information offered in the dictionary.

This need of the user gives the lexicographer a normative responsibility that compels him to include the 'correct' form or meaning, but it also compels him to include and pass judgement on 'incorrect' forms. These judgemental findings of the lexicographer have to be included in the dictionary entries as separate sections and they constitute yet another information category. Lexicographical comments on incorrect forms can also be regarded as a feature of more advanced dictionaries. Afrikaans dictionaries still fail to respond to this challenge in an effective way.

Language teachers have an occupational devotion to dictionaries and they should be regarded as one of the most active user groups of general monolingual and translation·dictionaries. A purist urge amongst Afrikaans language teachers has led to a well-established resistance to the use of so-called 'Anglicisms' in Afrikaans. This attitude has a historical motivation. The struggle for the recognition of Afrikaans as official language alongside English has resulted in an excessive sensitivity to any form of English influence on Afrikaans and, in particular, on the lexicon. This attitude has had a definite impact on Afrikaans dictionaries.

Today the same degree of sensitivity does not prevail any longer, but there still exists a strong purist urge. This purist resistance does not, however, reflect the general attitude towards linguistic borrowing from English. Due to persistent language contact, the Afrikaans vocabulary includes a sizeable amount of words that are either direct translations from English or English loan words. In everyday Afrikaans these forms occur very frequently. The purist resistance is not aimed at all these borrowings or direct translations, but merely at those lexical items that are assumed to endanger the use of existing 'pure' Afrikaans forms. Such forms of English origin are stigmatized as 'Anglicisms'.

Contrary to the attitude regarding Anglicisms, loan words that do not substitute or oust existing Afrikaans forms are normally welcomed into the lexicon. The lexicographical treatment of these loan words refers to their English origin in a way similar to those from any other language. Lemmas like *rugby* and *speaker* 'chairman of a lawmaking body' get the label E in the NASIONALE WOORDEBOEK to indicate their English origin. This labelling runs parallel to that of, for example, *charade* F (French) or *confetti* It. (Italian). As a segment of the Afrikaans vocabulary these words are treated without any indication of a purist bias. These different attitudes towards Anglicisms and other loan words are clearly indicated by the editors of the NASIONALE WOORDEBOEK in the guide to their dictionary. By labelling a lemma as Ang., the NASONALE WOORDEBOEK says that the word is used under the influence of English and that its use is disapproved of in 'polished' style. On the other hand, many words of foreign origin are accepted in Afrikaans for technical or other reasons and are labelled according to the language of origin without any stigmatization.

The purist urge in Afrikaans dictionaries results in a definite Anglicist bias. Contrary to other loan words these lemmas do not have a neutral label to indicate their English origin, but they are marked as Ang. (Anglicism), and by doing so the lexicographer casts his disapproval over them. Although the dictionary recognizes these words as elements of the Afrikaans lexicon, their stigmatization is clearly indicated. The way in which the NASIONALE WOORDEBOEK treats the lemmas *geskeduleer* (scheduled) and *partisie* (partition) gives clear evidence of this:

> *geskeduleer* "... (Angl.) wat in 'n skedule opgeneem is. ... vaste, gereelde dienste"
> *partisie* "... 3. (Angl.) skeidsmuur, tussenskot."

Both these articles not only include the Anglicism as entry, but a cross-reference to the proper Afrikaans variant: *vaste/gereelde* and *skeidsmuur, tussenskot*.

From a normative point of view, this seems to be the application of a sound principle: labelling the less proper form and supplementing it with a cross-reference to the approved form. The labelling of Anglicisms does not only constitute part of the overall policy to employ labels where a deviation from the standard language has to be marked; it also establishes the presentation of a separate microstructural category, i.e., normative information.

As instruments of language usage, dictionaries should display an ample amount of normative information and this category should include a wide variety of prescriptive entries. The standardization of language is subjected to the application of different types of norms (cf. Carstens 1989), and the lexicographer should reflect the application of these norms. However, the normative category in Afrikaans dictionaries displays an uneven coverage of the various applicable norms, emphasizing the aims of the purist urge to bar all Anglicisms from the collection of approved members of the Afrikaans lexicon. This purist bias leads to the neglect of much other relevant normative information.

The need for prescriptive information has served as motivation for the publication of several special-purpose dictionaries dealing exclusively with lemmas that need a judgemental treatment. These 'restricted' dictionaries give a detailed treatment of a wide variety of normative issues. The existence of these dictionaries can be regarded as an attempt by the lexicographer to rectify the uneven coverage of normative information in general monolingual dictionaries. The leading representative of this dictionary type is DIE KORREKTE WOORD.

As is the case with general dictionaries, DIE KORREKTE WOORD supplies information on the Anglicist status of lemmas; for example, the article of the lemma *meer of min* (more or less) only contains the following entry: "Anglisisme vir: *min of meer*" It is marked as an Anglicism and supplemented with the correct Afrikaans equivalent. DIE KORREKTE WOORD differs from other dictionaries in the treatment of Anglicisms because it does not only mark the particular lemma as an Anglicism with a cross-reference to the appropriate Afrikaans form, but quite often it also comments on the usage of the Afrikaans lexical item in question. This kind of information transfer is lacking in most general monolingual dictionaries. The lexical items *een en almal* (one and all) and *eventueel* (eventual) are not included in desk dictionaries like the NASIONALE WOORDEBOEK and the VERKLARENDE HANDWOORDEBOEK VAN DIE AFRIKAANSE TAAL. Their omission is due to the fact that purists regard them as Anglicisms. DIE KORREKTE WOORD treats the lemma *een en almal* as follows:

> "'n Gevestigde Anglisisme" (an established Anglicism).

The transfer of information is far more comprehensive than if the item had been merely omitted.

Afrikaans does have a word *eventueel* with the meaning 'possible'. In desk dictionaries the entry on *eventueel* only includes this meaning, without any reference to the meaning 'eventual'. The meaning 'eventual' is lexicalised as *uiteindelik* in Afrikaans. DIE KORREKTE WOORD treats the lemma *eventueel* as follows:

> "Daar word beweer dat *eventueel* in die sin van "uiteindelik" anglisisties is: ... Die woord, so word gesê, moet gebruik word in die sin van "moontlik, waarskynlik": ... Die stryd teen *eventueel* = "uiteindelik" lyk vrugteloos." (It is maintained that *eventueel* in the sense of "eventual" is Anglicist: ... The word, so it is professed, should be used in the sense of "possible, probable": ... The struggle against *eventueel* = "eventual" appears to be futile.)

The search of the user looking for prescriptive advice regarding *eventueel* in general standard dictionaries will be in vain. An information category that should be covered receives no attention in a type of dictionary that is supposed to help its user in this matter. In DIE KORREKTE WOORD the user is rewarded with a comprehensive information package. Not only is the lexical item included and marked as an Anglicism with a cross-reference to the approved Afrikaans form, but the lexicographer also indicates that *eventueel* is winning the struggle for recognition - although general recognition is still due. By giving this information, the dictionary is not only extending its prescriptive function, but also reflecting the linguistic reality and the status of a specific lexical item as an element of the Afrikaans lexicon.

Although general monolingual dictionaries also include normative information regarding Anglicisms, their coverage of this information type is not as comprehensive as that of DIE KORREKTE WOORD. The latter is a restrictive dictionary specializing in normative information and its treatment of this information type tends to be more comprehensive than that of other dictionaries. It also includes information regarding norms of orthography, pronunciation, lexical item status, morphology, language interference and lexical variants. The quality and comprehensiveness of this dictionary also accentuates the uneven coverage of this information type in general monolingual dictionaries of Afrikaans.

When it comes to the selection of macrostructural elements, Afrikaans dictionaries exhibit a definite word bias. Lexicographers adhere to the principle that dictionaries are 'wordbooks' that have to reflect the collection of words belonging to a specific language. But the lexicon of a language consists of items which can be words or elements smaller or larger than words.

Where the compilation of a dictionary is subjected to such a word bias, a detrimental influence on the coverage of information can be detected. By being only a wordbook, the dictionary fails in its most important aim, i.e. to present knowledge on a representative collection of lexical items. A word bias results in an unbalanced selection of lexical items, which leads to an uneven lexicographical reflection of the vocabulary, neglecting a sufficient account of sublexical and multilexical lemmas. Afrikaans has numerous lexical items that are not words but elements smaller or larger than words, and these items are not treated satisfactorily in dictionaries.

The advantages of a lexically based approach and the disadvantages of a word based approach will receive no further attention in this paper. (Further comments on this problem are made in Gouws forthcoming a and forthcoming b.)

*Conclusion*

Lexicographical activities in South Africa have resulted in the publication of numerous dictionaries in a variety of languages, covering a wide spectrum of information categories. Although these dictionaries display an uneven coverage, there is an increasing interest in the underlying linguistic and pragmatic principles. Proposals have been made and projects are under way to enhance the standard of South African dictionaries by improving the scope and nature of the information categories treated in the various dictionary types, monolingual and interlingual. This should lead to the production of dictionaries that can be used as adequate language instruments and suitable 'containers of knowledge' in the future.

# 7 The Organisation of Lexicography in Africa

by Reinhard Hartmann

*Introduction*

Papers **1** to **6** above sketch the lexicographic situation in different parts of Africa from the points of view of language, history, politics and technology, and in relation both to the contents and the use of dictionaries. But even taken together these regions and aspects do not add up to a complete picture. The task of surveying the state of lexicography overall will be undertaken here, starting with a description of the major geographical regions.

The brief is immense, and the difficulties are enormous, as such a survey has not been attempted before on this scale to my knowledge, and the information that would be required is widely scattered, sorely incomplete, astonishingly out of date, or simply not available at all. I have drawn on four main types of sources:

(a) structural data on individual countries (summarised in tabular form in Appendix **A**);

(b) State-of-the-art Reports submitted to the Exeter Workshop by participants and others (see Appendix **B**);

(c) bibliographical guides and other reference books (see Bibliography **8.1**);

(d) selected other publications (see Bibliography **8.3**).

As we shall see, the findings are very tentative. Rather than a complete directory of experts, achievements, projects and resources, we get a fragmentary catalogue of all the things we do not know (yet). But I believe nevertheless that even that modest realisation will be useful for determining future progress.

*The Five Major Regions*

The geographical extent is vast. Africa, the second largest continent, consists of 48 countries (counting Madagascar, but not the 9 smaller outlying island groups), several of which exceed even the largest European states in size. A closer look at some basic structural data for these countries (Appendix **A**) reveals wide discrepancies between large and small political units, between rich and poor societies, between tropical and moderate climates, etc. There are also considerable differences according to religious loyalties (e.g. Islamic vs. Christian faiths), linguistic-cultural affiliations (e.g. Bantu vs. Saharan, Francophone vs. Anglophone), etc.

It is almost impossible to generalise about what all these places and people have in common, except in the most abstract terms. We may note, for instance, that most of the countries are the result of recent negotiations following a period of anti-colonial rebellion during and after the late 1950's (Liberia and Ethiopia are exceptions in this respect). Because of their relatively sudden creation and short national history, most of these states have arbitrary boundaries; Manshard (1988:62) has claimed that only about a quarter of the territorial borders follow 'natural' (i.e. river or ethnic) dividing lines. Gross observation will also reveal similarities in governmental styles and economic conditions, with largely left-wing regimes attempting to control low-income societies, the average annual income per head being well below $·500 in most countries. The only organisation of which all 50 or so African states (except the Republic of South Africa) are members are the United Nations, with its Economic Commission for Africa, the Organization of African Unity, and the African Development Bank.

It is helpful, perhaps, to distinguish five regional groupings - some of which have been hinted at in other papers above - using a number of criteria.

In the 'North', stretching from the Mediterranian coast across the Atlas mountain range to the Sahara Desert, lie the 'Arab League' countries (from west to east) *Morocco*, *Algeria*, *Tunisia*, *Libya*, *Egypt* and *Sudan*, all with predominantly Muslim communities. The Islamic tradition is strong, but European influence from the colonial past lingers on, especially in the practices of the various educational systems. Arabic is typically the official language spoken (if not written) by the overwhelming majority of the population, the only notable competitors being French (especially in Algeria and Tunisia), Berber (especially in Morocco), and the Nilotic language Dinka (especially in Sudan).

In the largely sub-tropical savannahs of the 'West', south of the Sahara, lie the Atlantic coastal states of *Mauritania*, *Senegal*, *Gambia*, *Guinea-Bissau*, *Guinea*, *Sierra Leone*, *Liberia*, *Ivory Coast*, *Ghana*, *Togo*, *Benin* and *Nigeria* and the landlocked countries of *Mali*, *Burkina Faso*, *Niger* and *Chad*. Linguistically and culturally, this is a rather heterogeneous area, although its peoples share some experiences, e.g. a colonial past and adverse climatic and soil conditions, which have united them under the aegis of such bodies as the Niger Basin Authority, the Comité Permanent Inter-États de Lutte contre la Sécheresse dans le Sahel, and the Communauté Economique des États de l'Afrique de l'Ouest. European influence on political institutions (French, especially in the northern countries, and British, especially in Nigeria) can still be felt, and this indirectly also affects issues of individual language learning and national language planning. Many of the dozens of genetically affiliated Niger-Congo, Afro-Asiatic and Nilo-Saharan languages in the area (Pulaar-Fulfulde, Yoruba, Igbo, Hausa and Kanuri are the best-known examples) have yet to be described in detail. The picture is further complicated by the degree to which the non-indigenous religions of Christianity and Islam have overlaid more traditional belief systems, the permutations ranging from 100% Muslims in Mauritania in the Northwest to over 50% Christians in Ghana and Nigeria in the Southeast.

The third major region is 'Central' Africa, usually defined as consisting of the tropical forest nations (from northwest to southeast) *Cameroon*, the *Central African Republic*, *Guinea Equatorial*, *Gabon*, *Congo*, *Zaïre*, *Rwanda* and *Burundi*. As a result of missionary activities of the Belgians (in the Congo Basin), the British (in Cameroon) and the French (elsewhere), more than half of the population are reported to be Christians. European colonial administrators have also left their mark on the institutional framework of these countries. In 1983 the Communauté Economique des États de l'Afrique Centrale was set up by linking the Customs Union of the 5 western states and the Great Lakes Community of the 3 eastern states with two other countries outside the region. Of the diverse range of (largely Niger-Congo) languages, the most important are Fulfulde, Sango, Kongo, Luba, Lingala and the supraregional lingua franca kiSwahili.

The 'Eastern' region stretches from the Red Sea in the Northeast to the Kalahari Desert in the South and consists of the old empire (now people's republic) *Ethiopia*, the Arab League countries *Djibouti* and *Somalia*, and the equatorial and sub-tropical Great Rift Valley states *Uganda*, *Kenya*, *Tanzania*, *Malawi*, *Zambia*, *Zimbabwe* and *Botswana*. Some authorities also include the Lusophone countries of *Mozambique* on the Indian Ocean and *Angola* on the Atlantic coast (these are also part of the 9-nation South African Development Coordination Conference), and even the large island state of *Madagascar*.

The seven countries formerly under British administration together with the three Horn of Africa states constitute the so-called Preferential Trade Area for Eastern and Southern Africa (which also includes SWAPO/Namibia, Lesotho, Swaziland and some island groups, but not Madagascar). With the exception of the extreme North, the population in this area is predominantly Christian and Bantu-speaking (kiSwahili is particularly well-established in Tanzania, Kenya and Uganda); Afro-Asiatic languages like Amharic and Somali prevail in Ethiopia, Djibouti and Somalia; the Malayo-Polynesian language Malagasy is dominant in Madagascar.

The fifth and final group is the 'South', composed of the *Republic of South Africa* and the so-called '*Homelands*' (part of a wider Southern African Customs Union with Botswana, *Lesotho* and *Swaziland*) and *Namibia* (which is on the verge of independence and on the edge of the 'front line' opposition to apartheid). Three quarters of the population are Christian, the majority are speakers of Bantu languages such as siZulu. Afrikaans and English are also widely spoken (or at least understood) by both Whites and Blacks.

*Lexicographical Activities*

To answer the question of whether a pan-African approach to lexicography is possible or desirable, we must bear in mind the cultural-linguistic and political-economic background as sketched above. In particular, we must go on to ask whether the best of the old traditions can be strengthened by appropriate new institutions.

*Languages covered.* The number and distribution of languages in Africa certainly challenge the conventional Eurocentric view of communication as standardised monoglot discourse. In most African contexts, the equation "one language = one nation" does not exist: most countries manifest a multiplicity of languages none of which are 'naturally' dominant and 'nationally' standardised (cf. Alexandre 1971); many are in the form of flexible continua of unwritten dialects, and individual and collective multilingualism is widespread. Few indigenous tongues have achieved the full register range of international languages like English or French, which is why many countries have been unable to settle the issue of which language(s) should be accorded 'national' or 'official' status. In spite of low numbers of proficient speakers, French is still the official language in at least 18 Francophone states of Africa, English is similarly marked in 16 countries, Portuguese in three, and Spanish in one. Arabic is the official language in 9 countries, occasionally jointly with French. The only African languages given official status are kiSwahili (in Tanzania), seSotho (in Lesotho), seTswana (in Botswana), kiRundi (in Burundi), Amharic (in Ethiopia), kinyaRwanda (in Rwanda), Somali (in Somalia) and Malagasy (in Madagascar).

A relatively small number of other local languages have achieved what is sometimes called 'national' status: Umbundu in Angola; Moore in Burkina Faso; Sango in the Central African Republic; Kongo in Congo and Zaïre; Pulaar-Fulfulde in Guinea, Mali, Niger and Senegal; kiSwahili in Kenya, Uganda and Zaïre; chiNyanja-chiChewa in Zambia and Malawi; Hausa, Yoruba and Igbo in Nigeria; siSwati in Swaziland. However, their use is often restricted to the media and education within major administrative divisions of the countries in question (cf. Brann 1979), and hardly ever considered suitable for international communication.

The impact of European languages has produced a number of 'contact vernaculars', the study of which has recently become fashionable. The best-known of these are (English) Pijin in Cameroon and Krio in Sierra Leone, (Portuguese) Krioulo in Guinea-Bissau, and (French) Creole in Mauritius and other Indian Ocean islands. But in terms of native speaker numbers, these pale into insignificance in comparison with Afrikaans (Cape Dutch), for which over 5 million speakers have been claimed.

The linguistic situation as described above is reflected in the numbers and kinds of dictionaries that have been produced. Monolingual dictionaries are still rather rare, even for some of the 'official' and 'national' languages. Bilingual dictionaries with European languages seem to be the most highly developed type. According to Hendrix's valuable bibliography (1982), the league table of dictionaries is topped by the following languages:

1 kiSwahili (217 titles)
2 Amharic (175)
3 Arabic (135)
4 Afrikaans (92)
5 Berber (79)
6 siZulu-siXhosa-siSwati (75)

7 Hausa (71)
8 Oromo (70)
9 Somali (59)
10 Tigrinya (57)
11 Yoruba (52)
12 Mandinka-Bambara (50)

Thus, only 12 languages (less than a sixth of Africa's 85 languages of more than one million speakers, cf. Paper **1** above) account for 1,132 (or 44%) of the 2,570 dictionaries listed in Hendrix (1982)!

*Dictionary typology.* Many of these dictionaries are limited in size or quite old, being the work of early missionaries and colonial administrators. The list does not include all the official and national languages; most of the minor local languages have not been codified at all (cf. Ansre 1971), Andrzejewski 1974, Heine & Möhlig 1980, Manessy & Valdman 1981). A comprehensive history or typology of these dictionaries has yet to be written, notwithstanding the isolated studies for specific languages or language groups like Arabic (Nassar 1956, El-Badry 1986), Afrikaans (Gouws 1986), the Bantu languages (Benson 1964, Mbogho 1985, Fabian 1986), or Hausa (Newman 1974).

Some of the major landmarks in the history of African lexicography are mentioned in Papers **1** to **6** above, e.g. the LISAN AL-ᶜARAB (Ibn Manzur 13th century) and AL-ᶜMUᶜJAM AL-ᶜARABI AL-'ASASI (ALECSO 1988) for Arabic, the WOORDEBOEK VAN DIE AFRIKAANSE TAAL (Schoonees et al. from 1961) for Afrikaans, the KAMUSI YA KISWAHILI SANIFU (TUKI 1981) and the DICTIONNAIRE SWAHILI-FRANÇAIS (Lenselaer 1983) for kiSwahili. Very few multilingual and technical dictionaries have been compiled in Africa; out of over 2 1/2 thousand dictionaries listed in Hendrix (1982), only 107 are labelled 'polyglot' and 151 'special and classified'.

*Lexicographers.* There are no reliable estimates of how many dictionary makers are active in Africa today. Very few that have been reported, e.g. in the State-of-the-art Reports compiled for the Exeter Workshop, are African nationals working in lexicography full-time. Traditionally, compilers tended to be European missionaries and colonial administrators; more recently, anthropologists and linguists engaged in field-work have taken an interest in dictionary work. Language planning officials, translators, terminologists and university teachers also occasionally contribute to the enterprise, but projects often remain incomplete or partial because of limited resources and expertise (cf. Banjo & Young 1982, Louw 1985, Khamisi 1987).

*Institutions.* Very few of the 48 countries of Africa have a professional body specialising in lexicography, but several promote dictionary-making by other means. Some states in Northern Africa have academies, e.g. the Arabic Language Academy in Giza, the Ethiopian Language Academy in Addis Ababa, and the Somali Academy of Culture in Mogadishu. The Arab League Educational, Cultural and Scientific Organization in Rabat promotes lexicographic and terminological projects across national frontiers, but usually only involving Arabic.

Many countries support dictionary work through national language commissions or central ministries of (higher) education. Examples:

*Burkina Faso*: 'Commissions' for 11 languages;
*Cameroon*: 'Anthropological Research Centre' of the Ministry of Higher Education;
*Djibouti*: 'Institut Supérieur d'Études et de Recherches Scientifiques et Techniques';
*Ethiopia*: 'Institute of Nationalities';
*Nigeria*: 'Educational Research and Development Council';
*Republic of South Africa*: 'Human Science Research Council', 'Taalkommissie', 'Language Committees';
*Tanzania*: 'National Kiswahili Council';
*Togo*: 'Ewe Language Academy';
*Zaïre*: 'Centre de Recherches en Pédagogie Appliquée'.

Other countries finance projects directly through institutions of higher learning. Examples:

*Cameroon*: University centre at Yaounde;
*Libya*: University centres at Tripoli and Bengazi;
*Nigeria*: University centres at Kano, Zaria, Ibadan, Ife, Maiduguri and Imo;
*Senegal*: University centre at Dakar;
*Republic of South Africa*: University centres at Stellenbosch

and Pretoria;

*Tanzania*: University centres at Dar es Salaam (TUKI) and Zanzibar (EACROTANAL);

*Zaïre*: University centres at Kinshasa and Lubumbashi.

Agencies concerned with terminology (e.g. NTS at Pretoria, R.S.A., and ALECSO at Rabat, Morocco) provide standardised technical vocabulary for translation purposes, usually by means of computer data-bases (cf. Cluver 1989).

Valuable lexicographical spadework has been done by foreign foundations such as the Summer Institute of Linguistics/Société Internationale de Linguistique (SIL), e.g. at Yaounde in Cameroon, the Ghana Institute of Linguistics at Tamale, and the Centre d'Études Ethnologiques (CEEBA), e.g. at Bandundu in Zaïre, especially on previously unrecorded local languages (cf. also Rubin 1979).

*Publishers.* As resources for producing and markets for purchasing dictionaries are severely limited - and literacy rates are generally low - in most countries of Africa, publishers are reluctant to invest large sums in this genre. Government and academic presses are responsible for the publication of the results of scholarly dictionary projects, but commercial dictionary publishing is underdeveloped, except perhaps in the R.S.A. Some European publishers, especially from Britain and France, are influential in the production of materials related to the teaching of major foreign languages in schools and universities.

*Professional Societies.* There are at present no associations or societies of professional lexicographers. Such national or international bodies are likely to be created soon, possibly on the occasion of a major conference (see below), in countries where linguists already have established academic links, e.g. through the West African Languages Congress in Nigeria, the Société des Linguistes du Zaïre, and the S.A. Linguistic Society. A regional or even pan-African lexicography society is an urgent desideratum.

*Conferences.* Very few meetings have been held on exclusively lexicographical themes. Francophone countries have sponsored a number of conferences on problems of literacy and orthography at which the function of dictionaries has been discussed (e.g. Dumas et al. 1983).

Several national and international conferences and congresses of linguists specialising on African languages have taken place (in Nigeria, Zaïre, the R.S.A., Italy, and the U.S.A.), but lexicography has remained a minority subject. The Arab League has promoted at least one specialist meeting on the role of dictionaries in the 'Arabisation' process (Sabir 1981).

It is encouraging to report that in 1989 no fewer than five seminars were devoted to African lexicography in its relation to such fields as language learning and translation: at Exeter (March), at Stellenbosch (April), at Nsukka in Nigeria (August), at Zanzibar in Tanzania (July), and at Dar es Salaam in Tanzania (August).

*Series*. There are no periodicals or monograph series dedicated solely to lexicography in Africa. Journals covering the study of African languages (such as *Kiswahili*) occasionally include papers on the compilation, history, typology and use of dictionaries, but much more needs to be done to encourage this activity.

*Training*. Finally, and most importantly for the long-term development of lexicography in Africa, the subject of systematic training must be stressed. It is only by a combination of academic study and research as well as the sharing of practical experience that public awareness of the problems of dictionary production and use can be encouraged.

The role of conferences and publishing in the dissemination of knowledge has already been described; however, these processes will only be effective if they are backed by better training facilities. Very few higher education establishments in Africa provide such lexicographic training, which is why graduates often have to travel long distances for their higher studies abroad where they would join others specialising in this field (cf. titles of research theses by Monsen 1972, Caney 1984, Shephardson 1986, Bwenge 1988). There are at least ten potential components for training courses in lexicography:

1 'recording' (delimitation, gathering and processing of lexical data, including fieldwork and/or corpus collection),
2 'description' (analysis, structuring and arrangement of processed material, including definition work),
3 'presentation' (preparation of material for publication, taking account of target users' needs),
4 planning and organisation (including finance),

5 procedures and tools (including computing),
6 reflection and experimentation,
7 history of dictionary-making,
8 dictionary typology,
9 dictionary criticism,
10 dictionary use,

supplemented by reference to various contributing theoretical disciplines (such as linguistics and information technology) and strengthened by practical hands-on experience.

As a necessary preliminary to all this, better libraries and more textbooks are urgently needed (cf. Naden 1977, Swanepoel 1989).

# 8 Bibliography

## 8.1 *General Reference Works Consulted*

Anon. (1986/87) *Catalogue of Technical Dictionaries/Katalogus van Vakwoordeboeke*. Pretoria: National Terminology Services, Department of National Education [98 Afrikaans and/or English glossaries]

Anon. (1989) *Africa South of the Sahara 1990*. London: Europa Publications [19th ed.]

Anon. (1989) *The Middle East and North Africa 1989*. London. Europa Publications [35th ed.]

Berman, Jean-Pierre ed. (1983) *Le Guide des Langues. Méthodes et programmes*. Paris: BPI/CIREEL & Groupe Tests

Campbell, James ed. (1983) *World Dictionaries in Print 1983. A Guide to General and Subject Dictionaries in World Languages*. New York & London: R.R. Bowker

Collison, Robert L. et al. eds. (from 1978) *World Bibliographical Series*. Oxford: Clio Press
[over 90 volumes, including several on African countries]

Comrie, Bernard ed. (1987) *The World's Major Languages*. London & Sydney: Croom Helm

Dalby, David (1977) *Language Map of Africa and the Adjacent Islands*. London: International African Institute

Ghali, W.R. (1971) *Arabic Dictionaries. An Annotated Comprehensive Bibliography*. Cairo: Al-Hay'ah Al-Misriyyah Al-ᶜAmmah Lil-Kitab

Grimes, Barbara F. ed. (1988) *Ethnologue. Languages of the World.* Dallas TX: Summer Institute of Linguistics [with Index, 11th ed.]

Haefs, Hanswilhelm ed. (1988) *Der Fischer Weltalmanach '89. Zahlen - Daten -Fakten.* Frankfurt: Fischer TBV

Hendrix, Melvin K. (1982) *An International Bibliography of African Lexicons.* Metuchen NJ & London: Scarecrow Press

Mann, Michael & Dalby, David (1987) *A Thesaurus of African Languages. A Classified and Annotated Inventory of the Spoken Languages of Africa. With an Appendix on Their Written Representation.* London: H. Zell & K.G. Saur

Manshard, Walther (1970/88) *Afrika - südlich der Sahara* (Fischer Länderkunde 5). Frankfurt: Fischer TBV

Meier, Wilma ed. (1984) *Bibliography of African Languages.* Wiesbaden: O. Harrassowitz

Rubin, Joan (1979) *Directory of Language Planning Organizations.* Honolulu HI: East-West Center

## **8.2** *Cited Dictionaries*

Only those dictionaries are listed here (in alphabetical order of languages and titles) which are mentioned in the papers above, but not included in the bibliography by Hendrix (1982).

### Afar

(AN) AFAR-ENGLISH-FRENCH DICTIONARY (with Grammatical Notes in English)
Enid M. Parker & R.J. Hayward. London: School of Oriental and African Studies 1985

**Afrikaans**

DICTIONARY OF TERMINOGRAPHY/TERMINOGRAFIE-WOORDEBOEK
A.D. de V. Cluver. Pretoria: Human Sciences Research Council 1989

IDIOMEWOORDEBOEK. VERKLARINGS MET AFSONDERLIKE AFRIKAANSE EN ENGELSE BEGRIPPELYSTE
Meyer de Villiers & Rufus H. Gouws. Kaapstad: NASOU 1988

(DIE) KORREKTE WOORD
Henderik J.J.M. van der Merwe & Friedrich A. Ponelis. Pretoria: J.L. van Schaik [6th ed.] 1982

NASIONALE WOORDEBOEK
Meyer de Villiers et al. Kaapstad: NASOU [7th ed.] 1987

PATRIOT WOORDEBOEK AFRIKAANS-ENGELS/DICTIONARY OF CAPE DUTCH-ENGLISH
D.F. du Toit. Paarl: D.F. du Toit 1902

VERKLARENDE HANDWOORDEBOEK VAN DIE AFRIKAANSE TAAL
Francois F. Odendal et al. Doornfontein: Perskor [2nd ed.] 1979

[see also the NTS Catalogue of Technical Dictionaries (1986/87)

**Amharic**

ADDIS YAMAREÑÑA MÄZGÄBÄ QALAT [New Amharic Dictionary]
Dästa Täklä Wäld Zähagärä Wägda. Addis Ababa 1970

AMHARIC-ENGLISH DICTIONARY
Amsalu Aklilu. Addis Ababa: Kuraz Publishers 1987

**Arabic**

DICTIONNAIRE DE MÉDECINE FRANÇAIS-ARABE
Mahmoud Rushdi Al-Baqli. Paris: Imprimerie Orientale V. Goupy 1870

ELIAS' MODERN DICTIONARY ARABIC-ENGLISH
Elias A. Elias. Cairo: Elias Modern Press 1922/81

ELIAS' MODERN DICTIONARY ENGLISH-ARABIC
Elias A. Elias. Cairo: Elias Modern Press 1913/54

(AN) ENGLISH-ARABIC DICTIONARY OF MEDICINE, BIOLOGY AND ALLIED SCIENCES
Mohammad Sharaf. Cairo: Government Press [2nd ed.] 1928

FIQH AL-LUGHAH WA ASRAR AL-$^{c}$ARABIYYAH
Abu Mansur $^{c}$Abd Al-Malik Ibn Muhammad Al-Tha$^{c}$alibi. Cairo: Mustafa Al-Babi Al-Halabi 1900, reprint Beirut: Dar Maktabat Al-Hayah 1980

KITAB AL-$^{c}$AIN
Al-Khalil Ibn Ahmad, c. 780, reprint Baghdad: Matba$^{c}$at Al-$^{c}$Ani 1967

KITAB AL-BARI$^{c}$
Abu $^{c}$Ali Isma$^{c}$il Ibn Al-Qasim Al-Qali, c. 1000, reprint ed. Hashim Al-Ta$^{cc}$an. Baghdad: Maktabat Al-Nahdah 1975

LISAN AL-$^{c}$ARAB
Muhammad Ibn Mukarram Ibn Manzur, 13th cent., reprint Beirut: Dar Sadir 1965

LISAN AL-$^{c}$ARAB AL-MUHIT
Muhammad Ibn Mukarram Ibn Manzur 13th cent., reprint ed. Yusuf Khayyat & Nadim Mar$^{c}$ashli. Beirut: Dar Lisan Al-$^{c}$Arab 1970

MADD AL-QAMUS. AN ARABIC-ENGLISH LEXICON
E.W. Lane. London: Williams and Norgate 1863-93, reprint Beirut: Librairie du Liban 1968

(AL-) MUHKAM WA AL-MUHIT AL-A$^{c}$ZAM FI AL-LUGHAH
Abu Al-Qasim Ibn Sidah c. 1066, reprint Cairo: Ma$^{c}$had Al-Makhtutat al-$^{c}$Arabiyyah 1958-72

(AL-) MU$^{c}$JAM AL-$^{c}$ARABI AL-'ASASI LAROUSSE
ALECSO. Tunis: Larousse Nathan International 1988

(AL-) MU$^{c}$JAM AL-JADID LIL-TULLAB
Ali Ibn Hadiyah et al. Tunis: Al-Sharikah Al-Tunisiyyah Lil-Tawzi$^{c}$ [5th ed.] 1984

(AL-) MU$^{c}$JAM AL-WASIT
Ibrahim Mustafa et al. [Academy of the Arabic Language]. Cairo: Dar Al-Ma$^{c}$arif [2nd ed.] 1972

(AL-) MUKHASSAS
Abu Al-Qasim Ibn Sidah, c. 1066, reprint Bulaq: Al-Matba$^{c}$ah Al-Amiriyyah 1898-1903, Beirut: Al-Maktab Al-Tijari 1966

MUKHTASAR AL-$^{c}$AIN
Abu Bakr Al-Zubaidi c. 989 [unpublished]

(AL-) MUNAJJAD
Ali Ibn Al-Hasan Kura$^{c}$ Al-Naml, c. 930, reprint ed. A.H. $^{c}$Umar & D. $^{c}$Abd Al-Baqi. Cairo: $^{c}$Alam Al-Kutub 1976

PETIT DICTIONNAIRE ARABE-FRANÇAIS DE LA LANGUE PARLÉE EN ALGÉRIE
Bel Kassem ben Sedira. Alger: Jourdan 1902

(AL-) QAMUS AL-MUHIT
Muhammad Ibn Ya$^{c}$qub Al-Firuzabadi, c. 1415, reprint Beirut: Al-Mu'assasah Al-$^{c}$Arabiyyah Lil-Tiba$^{c}$ah wa Al-Nashr [no date]

QAMUS SA[c]ADEH [English-Arabic]
Khalil Sa[c]adeh. Cairo: Al-Jaridah Press 1911, reprint Beirut: Librairie du Liban 1974

SPOKEN ARABIC SELF-TAUGHT [Libyan vernacular]
Ahmed M. Ashiurakis. Tripoli: Libyan Press 1972

(AL-) SULLAM AL-KABIR [Lingva aegyptiaca restitvta]
Abu Al-Barakat Ibn Kabar, c. 14th cent., reprint ed. Athanasius Kircher. Roma: H. Scheus 1643/1848

(AL-) SULLAM AL-KANA'ISI
Yuhanna Al-Samannudi c. 13th cent., reprint Cairo: Imprimerie de l'Institut Français d'Archéologie Orientale 1930

TAJ AL-[c]ARUS
Murtada al-Zabidi 18th cent., reprint Kuwait: The Kuwaiti Government Press 1965-

(AL-) TALKHIS FI MA[c]RIFAT ASMA' AL-ASHYA'
Abu Hilal Al-[c]Askari, c. 1010, reprint ed. [c]Izzat Hasan. Damascus: Majma[c] Al-Lughah Al-[c]Arabiyyah 1969

**iciBemba**

BEMBA CLASSIFIED VOCABULARY
E. Hoch [W.F.]. Ilondola: Language Centre 1964

**Créole see Kreol**

**English**

CHAMBERS UNIVERSAL LEARNERS' DICTIONARY
Elizabeth M. Kirkpatrick. Edinburgh: W. & R. Chambers 1980

COLLINS COBUILD ENGLISH LANGUAGE DICTIONARY
John M. Sinclair et al. London and Glasgow: Collins 1987

COLLINS DICTIONARY OF THE ENGLISH LANGUAGE
Patrick Hanks et al. London and Glasgow: Collins 1979

COLLINS-ROBERT SCHOOL FRENCH-ENGLISH, ENGLISH-FRENCH DICTIONARY
B.T. Atkins et al. London and Glasgow: Collins 1983

LONGMAN DICTIONARY OF CONTEMPORARY ENGLISH
Della Summers. Harlow: Longman [2nd ed.] 1987

LONGMAN PRIMARY DICTIONARY
Della Summers. Harlow: Longman 1985

OXFORD ADVANCED LEARNERS'DICTIONARY
A.S. Hornby with A.P. Cowie. Oxford: U.P. [3rd ed.] 1974

OXFORD ENGLISH DICTIONARY
J. Murray et al./W.A. Craigie & C.T. Onions/R.W. Burchfield. Oxford: Clarendon Press/Oxford U.P. 1884-1933/1972-1986 [2nd ed. 1989]

[see also *Afrikaans, Arabic, Igbo, Lingala, kiSwahili, siZulu*]

**French**

DICTIONNAIRE DU FRANÇAIS CONTEMPORAIN
Jean Dubois et al. Paris: Larousse [2nd ed.] 1971

COLLINS-ROBERT SCHOOL FRENCH-ENGLISH, ENGLISH-FRENCH DICTIONARY
B.T. Atkins et al. London and Glasgow: Collins 1983

[see also *Arabic, Lingala, kiSwahili*]

**French Creole see Kreol**

**Hausa**

LEXIQUE SCIENTIFIQUE FRANÇAIS-HAUSA
Issoufou Mahamane. Niamey 1982

**Havu**

DESCRIPTION DE LA LANGUE HAVU (BANTOU J52). GRAMMAIRE ET LEXIQUE [2 volumes]
B. Aramazani. Bruxelles: Université Libre de Bruxelles [Ph.D.] 1985

**Igbo**

IGBO-ENGLISH DICTIONARY
Kay Williamson. Benin City: Ethiope Publ. Corporation 1972

**Kreol**

DIKSYONER KREOL MORISYEN/DICTIONARY OF MAURITIAN CREOLE/DICTIONNAIRE DU CRÉOLE MAURICIEN
Philip Baker & Vinesh Y. Hookoomsing. Paris: L'Harmattan 1987

**Lingala**

LINGALA GRAMMAR AND DICTIONARY ENGLISH-LINGALA, LINGALA-ENGLISH
Malcolm Guthrie & John F. Carrington. London: Baptist Missionary Society 1988

MALOBA MA LOKOTA LINGALA/DICTIONNAIRE LINGALA. LINGALA-FRANÇAIS, FRANÇAIS-LINGALA
René van Everbroeck. Kinshasa: Editions l'Epiphanie 1985

**eMakua**

DICIONARIO MACUA-PORTUGUES
Anon. Nampula-Anchilo: Ediçao do Centro Catequético Paulo VI 1976

DICIONARIO PORTUGUES-MACUA
Pires Prata. Cucujªes: Sociedade Portuguesa das Missºes Católicas 1973

**Ronga-Tsonga**

TSONGA TERMINOLOGIE EN SPELREELS
Departmentele Tsonga Taalkomitee. Pretoria: Staatsdrukker 1972

**seSotho-seTswana**

BUKANTSWE YA MALEMO-PEDI SeSOTHO-SeAFRIKAANS/ TWEETALIG WOORDEBOEK AFRIKAANS-SUID-SOTHO
J.A. Du Plessis et al. Parow: Via Afrika 1974

GROOT NOORD-SOTHO WOORDEBOEK NOORD-SOTHO/ AFRIKAANS/ENGELS
D. Ziervogel. Pretoria: J.L. van Schaik [2nd ed.] 1985

PUKUNTSU. NOORD-SOTHO/AFRIKAANS, AFRIKAANS/NOORD-SOTHO WOORDEBOEK VOLGENS DIE JONGSTE ORTOGRAFIE OPGESTEL
Thomas J. Kriel. Pretoria: J.L. van Schaik [3rd ed.] 1983

SKOOLWOORDEBOEK SUID-SOTHO/AFRIKAANS, AFRIKAANS-SUID-SOTHO
C.R. Kok & L.C. Botha. Kaapstad: Juta 1978

TSWANA TERMINOLOGIE EN SPELREELS
Departmentele Tswana Taalkomitee. Pretoria: Staatsdrukker 1972

('N) WOORDEBOEK VAN TEMATOLOGIESVERWANTE WOORDE / (A) DICTIONARY OF THEMATICALLY RELATED WORDS / BUKANTSWE YA MAFOKO AMOGANANG LE DIDIRISO
W.J. Wright. Johannesburg: Educum 1987

**kiSwahili**

DICTIONNAIRE DES ETUDIANTS FRANÇAIS-SWAHILI, SWAHILI-FRANÇAIS
Irène Monot-Chopard. Nyankunde, Bunia: Editions Evangéliques 1969

DICTIONNAIRE SWAHILI-FRANÇAIS
Alphonse Lenselaer. Paris: Editions Karthala 1983

KAMUSI/VOCABULAIRE FRANÇAIS-KISWAHILI, KISWAHILI-FRANÇAIS
Walter Heylen. Lubumbashi: Editions Saint Paul 1985

KAMUSI YA KISWAHILI SANIFU
TUKI. Dar es Salaam & Nairobi: Oxford U.P. 1981

LEARNER'S SWAHILI-ENGLISH, ENGLISH-SWAHILI DICTIONARY
Ali Ahmed Jahadhury. London: Evans Brothers 1981

LEXIQUE TEMBO I [Tembo-Swahili du Zaire-Japonais-Français]
S. Kaji. Tokyo: Institute for the Study of Languages and Cultures of Asia and Africa 1985

(LE) PLUS ANCIEN DICTIONNAIRE BANTU. VOCABULARIUM P. GEORGII GELENSIS
[1651-52] reprint ed. J. van Wing & C. Penders. Louvain: Bibliothèque Congo 1928

(A) SHORT ENGLISH-SWAHILI MEDICAL DICTIONARY
T.H. White. Edinburgh: Livingstone 1979

SWAHILI GRAMMAR, VOCABULARY AND PHRASES
G.M. Jardine. Kampala: Uganda Printing 1920

**Tembo see kiSwahili**

**siZulu-siXhosa-siSwati**

AFRIKAANS-ZULU, ZULU-AFRIKAANS WOORDEBOEK / ENGLISH-ZULU, ZULU-ENGLISH DICTIONARY
Tegnidisc. Goodwood: Oudiovista 1984

XHOSA DICTIONARY ENGLISH-XHOSA-AFRIKAANS, XHOSA-ENGLISH-AFRIKAANS
H.L. Nabe et al. King Williamstown: Educum 1976

### 8.3 *Other Literature*

This list includes all references to secondary sources mentioned in the papers above other than general reference works (8.1) and dictionaries (8.2).

Alberts, Mariëtta & Mtintsilana, Priscilla (1988) *Leksikografiese ontleding van Afrikaanse en Afrikatale-leksikons*. Pretoria: Raad vir Geesteswetenskaplike Navorsing

Alexandre, Pierre (1961) "Problèmes linguistiques des états négro-africains à l'heure de l'indépendance"
2: 69-91

———— (1971) "Multilingualism" in Sebeok et al. (1971) 537-549

———— (1972) *An Introduction to Languages and Language in Africa*. London: Heinemann

Al-Kasimi, Ali M. (1977) *Linguistics and Bilingual Dictionaries*. Leiden: E.J. Brill

Al-Sufi, A. (1986) *Al-Lughah wa Ma*ᶜ*ajimuha fi Al-Maktabah Al-*ᶜ*Arabiyyah*. Damascus: Tallas

Andrzejewski, B.W. (1974) "The introduction of a national orthography for Somali" *African Language Studies* 15: 199-203

Ansre, Gilbert (1971) "Language standardisation in Sub-Saharan Africa" in Sebeok et al. (1971) 680-698

Bakalla, M.H. (1983) *Arabic Linguistics. An Introduction and Bibliography*. London: Mansell

Banjo, A. & Young, P. (1982) "On editing a second-language dictionary: the proposed Dictionary of West African English (DWAE)" *English World-wide* 3: 87-91

Barreteau, Daniel ed. (1978) *Inventaire des études linguistiques sur les pays d'Afrique noire d'expression française et sur Madagascar*. Paris: CILF

Bender, M. Lionel ed. (1983) *Nilo-Saharan Language Studies*. East Lansing MI: Michigan State University African Studies Center

Bennett, P.R. (1986) "Grammar in the lexicon: two Bantu cases" *Journal of African Languages and Linguistics* 8, 1: 1-30

Benson, T.G. (1964) "A century of Bantu lexicography" *African Language Studies* 5: 64-91

Brann, C.M.B. (1979) "A typology of language education in Nigeria" in *Language and Society* ed. W.C. McCormack & S.A. Wurm. The Hague: Mouton 463-507

Brosnahan, L.F. (1963) "Some aspects of the linguistic situation in Tropical Africa" *Lingua* 12: 54-65

Bwenge, Charles M.T. (1988) *Affixational Morphology and Dictionary Design. A Case Study of Swahili Lexicography*. Exeter University [M.Phil.]

Caney, John (1984) *The Modernisation of Somali Vocabulary, with Particular Reference to the Period 1972 to the Present*. Hamburg: H. Buske [Ph.D. London SOAS]

Carstens, Willem A.M. (1989) *Norme vir Afrikaans*. Cape Town: Academica

CELTA ed. (1974) *Actes du 1er Séminaire des Linguistes du Zaïre*. Lubumbashi: CELTA

Cluver, A.D. de V. (1989) *A Manual of Terminography*. Pretoria: Human Sciences Research Council

Cole, Desmond T. (1971) "The history of African linguistics to 1945" in Sebeok et al. (1971) 1-29

Collison, Robert L. (1982) *A History of Foreign-Language Dictionaries*. London: A. Deutsch

Coupez, A. (1975) "La variabilité lexicale en bantou" *African Languages/Langues Africaines* 1: 164-203

——————— (1985) "Problèmes et méthodes en lexicographie bantoue" in *Guide de recherche en lexicographie et terminologie*. ed. A. Clas. Paris: Agence de Coopération Culturelle et Technique 99-112

Dalby, David (1967) "A survey of the indigenous scripts of Liberia, Sierra Leone: Vai, Mende, Loma, Kpelle and Bassa" *African Language Studies* 8: 1-51

——————— (1968) "The indigenous scripts of West Africa and Surinam: their inspiration and design" *African Language Studies* 9: 156-197

——————— (1969) "Further indigenous scripts of West Africa: Manding, Wolof and Fula asphabets and Yoruba 'holy' writing" *African Language Studies* 10: 161-181 [including postscript on Gola]

——————— ed. (1970) *Language and History in Africa*. London: F. Cass

De Jonghe, E. (1933) "Les missions religieuses au Congo Belge" *Congo: Revue Générale de la Colonie Belge* [Janvier] 1-24

Diringer, David (1949) *The Alphabet*. London & New York: Hutchinson

Doke, Clement M. (1931) *Report on the Unification of the Shona Dialects*. Salisbury: Government of Southern Rhodesia

Dubois, Jean (1981) "Models of the dictionary: evolution in dictionary design" *Applied Linguistics* 2,3: 236-249

Dumas, G. et al. eds. (1983) *Conférence des Ministres de l'Education des pays d'expression Française*. Québec: Ministère de l'Education

El-Badry, Nawal H. (1986) "The development of the bilingual English-Arabic dictionary from the middle of the 19th century to the present" in Hartmann (1986) 57-63

Fabian, Johannes (1986) *Language and Colonial Power*. Cambridge: U.P.

Faik, S. (1975) *Le Zaïre: deuxième pays francophone du monde?* Lubumbashi: CELTA

Foster, Phillip J. (1971) "Problems of literacy in Sub-Saharan Africa" in Sebeok et al. (1971) 587-617

Gouws, Rufus H. (1986) "Afrikaans lexicography" in Hartmann 75-83

——————— (1989) Leksikografie. Cape Town: Academica

——————— (forthcoming) "Setsels as makrostruktuurelemente van Afrikaanse woordeboeke" *S.A. Tydskrif vir Taalkunde*

Greenberg, Joseph H. (1963) *Languages of Africa* (Publications of the Research Center in Anthropology, Folklore and Linguistics 25). Bloomington: Indiana University

Hair, P.E.H. (1970) "The contribution of early linguistic material to the history of West Africa" in Dalby (1970) 50-63

Hartmann, R.R.K. ed. (1983) *Lexicography. Principles and Practice.* London: Academic Press

——————— ed. (1986) *The History of Lexicography*. Amsterdam: J. Benjamins

Haugen, Einar (1985) "Lexicography and language planning" in *Scientific and Humanistic Dimensions of Language* ed. K.R. Jankowsky. Amsterdam: J. Benjamins 571-580

Hausmann, F.J. (1981) "Wörterbücher und Wortschatzlernen" *Linguistik und Didaktik* 45/46: 71-78

Hausmann, F.J. et al. eds. (forthcoming) *Wörterbücher/Dictionaries/ Dictionnaires. International Encyclopedia of Lexicography*. Berlin: W. de Gruyter [Vol. I 1989]

Haywood, John A. (1960) *Arabic Lexicography*. Leiden: E. Brill

——————— (forthcoming) "Arabic lexicography" [Art. 237] in Hausmann et al.

Heestermans, Hans (forthcoming) "Niederländische und afrikaanse Lexikographie" [Art. 201] in Hausmann et al.

Heine, Bernd (1977) "Horizontal and vertical communication in Africa" *Afrika Spectrum* 12,3: 231-238

Heine, Bernd & Möhlig, Wilhelm J.G. (1980) *Language and Dialect Atlas of Kenya* [Vol. I]. Berlin: D. Reimer

Householder, Fred W. & Saporta, Sol eds. (1962) *Problems in Lexicography*. Bloomington: Indiana U.P.

Kadima, K. et al. (1983) *Atlas linguistique du Zaïre: Inventaire préliminaire*. Paris: ACCT-CERDOTOLA

Khamisi, Abdu M. (1987) "Trends in Swahili lexicography" *Kiswahili* 54: 192-201

Louw, J.P. ed. (1985) *Lexicography and Translation*. Kaapstad: Bybelgenootskap van S.A.

MacWilliam, Anita M. (1984) "Research work in dictionary-making" *Kiswahili* 51: 102-110

Manessy, Gabriel & Valdman, Albert eds. (1981) *Les langues dans l'Afrique subsaharienne* (Les langues dans le monde ancien et moderne, ed. Manessy & Valdman, Vol. 1). Paris: Editions du CNRS

Mbogho, K. (1985) "Observations on bilingual lexicography involving Bantu and Indo-European languages" *Babel* 31, 3: 152-162

Mbula, Paluka (1981) *Répertoire des travaux de linguistique et de littérature orale de l'IPN[Kinshasa] 1965-1981, ISP[Gombe] 1967-1981* (Publications du CRPA 002, 003). Kinshasa

Mbulamoko, N.M. et al. (1986) *État d'utilisation des langues nationales (Kiluba, Kikongo, Kiswahili, Lingala) dans l'enseignement primaire et secondaire au Zaïre*. Kinshasa: UNESCO-CNR/IPN

McArthur, Tom (1986) *Worlds of Reference*. Cambridge: U.P.

Mdee, James S. (1984) "Constructing an entry in a learner's dictionary of Standard Kiswahili" in *LEXeter '83 Proceedings* ed. R.R.K. Hartmann (Lexicographica. Series Maior 1). Tübingen: M. Niemeyer 237-241

Meara, Paul (1983) *Vocabulary in a Second Language*. London: Centre for Information on Language Teaching and Research

Mkude, D.J. (1986) "English in contact with Swahili" in *English in Contact with Other Languages. Studies in Honour of Broder Carstensen on the Occasion of His 60th Birthday* ed. W. Viereck & W.-D. Bald. Budapest: Akadémiai Kiadó 513-532

Monsen, Randall B. (1972) *Semantic Preliminaries to Lexicography: A Study of the Hausa Verb*. New York: Columbia University [Ph.D.]

Naden, Anthony J. (1977) *Words and Meanings. A Guide to Practical Dictionary Work*. Tamale: Ghana Institute of Linguists

Nassar, H. (1956) *Al-Mu^c^jam Al-^c^Arabi: Nash'atuhu wa Tatawwuruhu* [2 volumes]. Cairo: Dar Misr Lil-Tiba'ah

Newman, Paul & Newman, Roxana Ma (forthcoming) "Lexicography of the Chadic Languages" [Art. 240] in Hausmann et al.
Newman, Roxana Ma (1974) "Dictionaries of the Hausa language" *Harsunan Nijeriya* 4: 1-25
Nwachukwu, A. (1971) "Igbo language studies: problems and principles" *CONCH* (Owerri) 3: 67-75
Osselton, Noel E. (1983) "The history of English language dictionaries" in Hartmann (1983) 13-22
Otto, Anna N. (forthcoming) *Kriteria vir 'n Afrikaanse aanlerderwoordeboek.* Stellenbosch University [D.Litt.]
Polomé, Edgar (forthcoming) "Lexicography of the Niger-Kordofanian Languages" [Art. 272] in Hausmann et al.
Quirk, Randolph (1986) "Opening remarks" in *Lexicography. An Emerging International Profession* ed. R.F. Ilson. Manchester: U.P. 1-6
Rubango, N.Y. (1986) "Le français au Zaïre: langue supérieure et chances de 'survie' dans un pays africain" *Language Problems and Language Planning* 10,3: 253-271
Sabir, Mohyi-el-Din ed. (1981) *The Arabic Dictionary* [Proceedings of ALECSO Symposium]. Rabat: Sahil Press
Schachter, Paul (1971) "The present state of African linguistics" in Sebeok et al. (1971) 30-44
Schoonees, Pieter C. (1958) *Rondom die Woordeboek.* Kaapstad: Nasionale Boekhandel
Sebeok, Thomas A. et al. eds. (1970) *Southwest Asia and North Africa* (Current Trends in Linguistics, Vol. 6). The Hague: Mouton
——————— (1971) *Linguistics in Sub-Saharan Africa* (Current Trends in Linguistics, Vol. 7). The Hague: Mouton
Séguy, Jean (1971) "La relation entre la distance spatiale et la distance lexicale" *Revue de linguistique romane* 35: 335-357
Shephardson, K.N. (1986) *Productivity and the Swahili Lexicon.* Bloomington: Indiana University [Ph.D.]
Snijman, Frederick J. (1980) "Thoughts on a dictionary of Afrikaans on historical principles" in *Proceedings of the Second International Round Table Conference on Historical Lexicography* ed. W.J.J. Pijnenburg & F. de Tollenaere. Dordrecht: Foris 333-347
Snoxall, R.A. (1965) "Some problems and principles of lexicography in Luganda" *African Language Studies* 6: 27-31
Spencer, John (1971) "Colonial language policies and their legacies"

in Sebeok et al. (1971) 537-547

——————— (1988) "Reflections on language and development in tropical Africa" in *Essays on the English Language and Applied Linguistics on the Occasion of Gerhard Nickel's 60th Birthday*, ed. J. Klegraf & D. Nehls. Heidelberg: J. Groos 479-488

Swanepoel, P.H. (1989) *Only Study Guide* [in Lexicography for] *Translation Studies (Honours)/Diploma in Translation*. Pretoria: University of South Africa

Tadadjeu, M. (1980) *A Model for Functional Trilingual Education Planning in Africa*. Paris: UNESCO

Temu, Canute W. (1984) "Kiswahili terminology: principles adopted for the enrichment of the Kiswahili language" *Kiswahili* 51: 112-126

Tucker, A.N. (1971) "Orthographic systems and conventions in Sub-Saharan Africa" in Sebeok et al. (1971) 618-653

ᶜUmar, Ahmad M. (1970) *Tarikh Al-Lughah Al-ᶜArabiyyah fi Misr*. Cairo: Al-Hay'ah Al-Misriyyah Al-ᶜAmmah Lil-Kitab

UNESCO (1951) *The Use of Vernacular Languages in Education* (Monographs on Fundamental Education 8). Paris: UNESCO

Wansbrough, John (1970) "Africa and the Arab geographers" in Dalby (1970) 89-101

Welmers, William E. (1971a) "Christian missions and language policies" in Sebeok et al. (1971) 559-569

——————— (1971b) "Checklist of African languages and dialect names" in Sebeok et al. (1971) 759-900

——————— (1973) *African Language Structures*. Berkeley: U. of California P.

Westermann, Diedrich & Bryan, M.A. (1970) *Handbook of African Languages* [Part II West African Languages]. Folkestone: Dawsons [1st ed. 1952. Ibadan: Oxford U.P. for International African Institute]

Whiteley, Wilfred H. (1971) "Language policies of independent African states" in Sebeok et al. (1971) 548-558

Yaᶜqub, Imil (1981) *Al-Maᶜajim Al-Lughawiyyah Al-ᶜArabiyyah: Bada'atuha wa Tatawwuruha*. Beirut: Dar Al-ᶜIlm Lil-Malayin

Appendix A: **Structural Data on African Countries**

Sources: for columns (1) & (2) Der Fischer Weltalmanach '89 (Haefs 1988)
for columns (3) & (4) Ethnologue. Languages of the World (Grimes 1988)
for column (5) A Thesaurus of African Languages (Mann & Dalby 1987)
for column (6) An International Bibliography of African Lexicons (Hendrix 1982)

| (1) | (2) | (3) | (4) | (5) | (6) |
|---|---|---|---|---|---|
| **COUNTRY** (Regime, date of independence) | **AREA** (1000 km²) **POPULATION** (million) | **LITERACY RATE** | **NUMBER OF** (living) **LANGUAGES** | **NAMES OF MAIN LANGUAGES** (speakers in population; *including second-language use) OL: official lg. | **NUMBER OF DICTIONARIES** |
| **Algeria** Dem. People's Republic, 1962 | 2,382<br>22.4 | 36% | 17 | Arabic OL (80%)<br>Berber (19%) | 135<br>79 |
| **Angola** People's Rep., 1975 | 1,247<br>9.0 | 15% | 42 | uMbundu (38%)<br>kiMbundu (27%) | 10<br>7 |
| **Benin** People's Rep. 1960 | 113<br>4.0 | 20% | 52 | Fon (26%) | 13 |
| **Botswana** Republic, 1966 | 600<br>1.2 | 40% | 26 | seTswana OL (90%) | 12 |

| **COUNTRY** (Regime, date of independence) | **AREA** (1000 km²) **POPULATION** (million) | **LITERACY RATE** | **NUMBER OF** (living) **LANGUAGES** | **NAMES OF MAIN LANGUAGES** (speakers in population; *including second-language use) OL: official lg. | **NUMBER OF DICTIONARIES** |
|---|---|---|---|---|---|
| **Burkina Faso**<br>Pres. Rep., 1960 | 274<br>6.8 | 12% | 72 | Moore (48%) | 14 |
| **Burundi**<br>Pres. Rep., 1962 | 28<br>4.9 | 18% | 3 | kiRundi OL (95%) | 11 |
| **Cameroon**<br>Pres. Rep., 1960 | 475<br>10.9 | 20% | 269 | Pijin Eng. (*20%)<br>Fulfulde (8%)<br>Ewondo (8%) | 5<br>49<br>6 |
| **Central African Republic**<br>Pres. Rep., 1960 | 623<br>2.7 | 20% | 105 | Gbaya-Manza (39%)<br>Banda (34%)<br>Sango (4%,*70%?) | 11<br>6<br>11 |
| **Chad**<br>Pres. Rep., 1960 | 1,284<br>5.1 | 12% | 117 | Arabic OL (14%)<br>Sara (19%) | 135<br>5 |
| **Congo**<br>People's Republic, 1960 | 342<br>1.8 | 40% | 57 | Kongo (50%)<br>Lingala (*20%?) | 36<br>20 |
| **Djibouti**<br>Pres. Rep., 1977 | 22<br>0.5 | 18% | 4 | Somali (36%) | 59 |

| COUNTRY<br>(Regime,<br>date of in-<br>dependence) | AREA<br>(1000 km²)<br>POPULATION<br>(million) | LITERACY RATE | NUMBER OF<br>(living)<br>LANGUAGES | NAMES OF MAIN LANGUAGES<br>(speakers in population;<br>*including second-language use)<br>OL: official lg. | NUMBER OF DICTIONARIES |
|---|---|---|---|---|---|
| **Egypt**<br>Pres. Rep., 1922 | 1,001<br>50.7 | 44% | 11 | Arabic OL (100%) | 135 |
| **Ethiopia**<br>Dem. People's Republic,<br>(1853) 1987 | 1,222<br>46.2 | 50% | 120 | Amharic OL (40%)<br>Oromo (27%)<br>Tigrinya (14%)<br>Somali (4%)<br>Welaita (4%)<br>Sidamo (3%) | 175<br>70<br>57<br>59<br>3<br>3 |
| **Gabon**<br>Pres. Rep., 1960 | 268<br>1.2 | 30% | 38 | Fang (35%) | 8 |
| **(The) Gambia**<br>Republic, 1965 | 11<br>0.7 | 10% | 19 | Mandinka (42%)<br>Pulaar (18%)<br>Wolof (16%) | 50<br>4<br>37 |
| **Ghana**<br>Republic, 1957 | 239<br>14.0 | 35% | 72 | Twi (29%)<br>Ewe (13%)<br>Fante (11%) | 18<br>44<br>18 |
| **Guinea Ecuatorial**<br>Pres. Rep., 1968 | 28<br>0.4 | 20% | 9 | Fang (68%) | 8 |

| COUNTRY (Regime, date of independence) | AREA (1000 km²) POPULATION (million) | LITERACY RATE | NUMBER OF (living) LANGUAGES | NAMES OF MAIN LANGUAGES (speakers in population; *including second-language use) OL: official lg. | NUMBER OF DICTIONARIES |
|---|---|---|---|---|---|
| **Guinea-Bissau** | 36 | 11% | 22 | Balanta (26%) | 2 |
| Republic, 1973 | 0.9 | | | Pulaar (23%) | 4 |
| | | | | Krioulo (*70%) | 5 |
| **Guinea** | 246 | 15% | 28 | Pulaar (40%) | 4 |
| Pres. Rep., 1958 | 6.3 | | | Mandinka (22%) | 50 |
| **Ivory Coast** | 322 | 32% | 72 | Baule (64%) | 5 |
| Pres. Rep., 1960 | 10.2 | | | Malinke-Dioula (61%) | 10 |
| | | | | Senufo (10%) | 1 |
| **Kenya** | 583 | 45% | 59 | kiSwahili (*65%) | 217 |
| Pres. Rep., 1963 | 22.9 | | | Gikuyu (20%) | 22 |
| | | | | English OL (*16%) | (not listed) |
| | | | | Luo (14%) | 11 |
| | | | | Luhya (13%) | 5 |
| | | | | kiKamba (11%) | 23 |
| | | | | Kalenjin (11%) | 8 |
| **Lesotho** | 30 | 71% | 4 | seSotho OL (99%) | 28 |
| Kingdom, 1966 | 1.6 | | | | |
| **Liberia** | 111 | 30% | 34 | English OL (?) | (not listed) |
| Pres. Rep., 1847 | 2.4 | | | | |

| COUNTRY (Regime, date of independence) | AREA (1000 km²) POPULATION (million) | LITERACY RATE | NUMBER OF (living) LANGUAGES | NAMES OF MAIN LANGUAGES (speakers in population; *including second-language use) OL: official lg. | NUMBER OF DICTIONARIES |
|---|---|---|---|---|---|
| **Libya**<br>People's Jamahiriya, 1951 | 1,760<br>3.7 | 37% | 11 | Arabic OL (95%) | 135 |
| **Madagascar**<br>Dem. Rep., 1960 | 587<br>10.3 | 44% | 3 | Malagasy OL (98%) | 47 |
| **Malawi**<br>Pres. Rep., 1964 | 118<br>7.5 | 26% | 14 | chiChewa (50%,*77%)<br>Yao (14%,*19%)<br>eMakua (15%) | 26<br>21<br>22 |
| **Mali**<br>Pres. Rep., 1960 | 1,240<br>8.7 | 11% | 23 | Mandinka-Bambara (80%)<br>Fulfulde (14%) | 53<br>49 |
| **Mauritania**<br>Pres. Rep., 1960 | 1,031<br>2.0 | 17% | 6 | Arabic OL (80%) | 135 |
| **Morocco**<br>Kingdom, 1956 | 447<br>22.5 | 24% | 9 | Arabic OL (65%)<br>Berber (38%) | 135<br>79 |
| **Mozambique**<br>People's Republic, 1975 | 802<br>14.6 | 24% | 24 | eMakua (38%)<br>Tsonga (24%)<br>Portuguese OL (*23%)<br>chiNyanja (13%) | 22<br>36<br>(not listed)<br>26 |

| COUNTRY (Regime, date of independence) | AREA (1000 km²) POPULATION (million) | LITERACY RATE | NUMBER OF (living) LANGUAGES | NAMES OF MAIN LANGUAGES (speakers in population; *including second-language use) OL: official lg. | NUMBER OF DICTIONARIES |
|---|---|---|---|---|---|
| **Namibia**<br>?, 1990 | 823<br>1.6 | 57% | 21 | oshiWambo (47%)<br>Afrikaans OL (14%) | 9<br>92 |
| **Niger**<br>Pres. Rep., 1960 | 1,267<br>6.1 | 8% | 18 | Hausa (80%)<br>Songhai (21%)<br>Fulfulde (14%) | 71<br>19<br>49 |
| **Nigeria**<br>Republic, 1960 | 924<br>98.5 | 30% | 413 | Hausa (21%,*38%)<br>Yoruba (20%,*25%)<br>Igbo (17%,*22%)<br>English OL (*10%)<br>Fulfulde (9%)<br>Efik (5%)<br>Kanuri (4%)<br>Tiv (3%)<br>Ijo (2%)<br>Edo (2%)<br>Nupe (1%) | 71<br>52<br>30<br>(not listed)<br>49<br>10<br>24<br>7<br>3<br>1<br>10 |
| Rwanda<br>Pres. Rep., 1962 | 26<br>6.3 | 25% | 3 | kinyaRwanda OL (*95%) | 11 |
| **Sahara**<br>Dem. Rep., ? | 266<br>0.2 | ? | ? | Arabic (?) | 135 (?) |

| COUNTRY (Regime, date of in-dependence) | AREA (1000 km²) POPULATION (million) | LITERACY RATE | NUMBER OF (living) LANGUAGES | NAMES OF MAIN LANGUAGES (speakers in population; *including second-language use) OL: official lg. | NUMBER OF DICTIONARIES |
|---|---|---|---|---|---|
| **Senegal**<br>Republic, 1960 | 196<br>6.6 | 10% | 37 | Wolof (80%)<br>Pulaar (21%)<br>French OL (15%) | 37<br>4<br>(not listed) |
| **Sierra Leone**<br>Pres. Rep., 1961 | 72<br>3.7 | 11% | 23 | Mende (31%)<br>Temne (30%) | 12<br>9 |
| **Somalia**<br>Republic, 1960 | 638<br>4.8 | 6% | 7 | Somali OL (98%) | 59 |
| **South Africa**<br>(inc. 'Homelands' Bophuthatswana, Ciskei, Transkei, Venda)<br>Fed. Rep., 1931, 1961 outside the Commonwealth | 1,221<br>33.8 | 50% | 32 | siZulu (22%)<br>isiXhosa (17%)<br>seSotho (7%)<br>seTswana (8%)<br>sePedi (9%)<br>Afrikaans OL (18%)<br>English OL (10%)<br>Tsonga (3%) | 53<br>29<br>28<br>12<br>14<br>92<br>(not listed)<br>23 |
| **Sudan**<br>Republic, 1956 | 2,506<br>22.2 | 20% | 135 | Arabic OL (50%)<br>Dinka (10%) | 135<br>11 |
| **Swaziland**<br>Kingdom, 1968 | 17<br>0.7 | 39% | 4 | siSwati (91%) | 4 |

| **COUNTRY** (Regime, date of in-dependence) | **AREA** (1000 km$^2$) **POPULATION** (million) | **LITERACY RATE** | **NUMBER OF** (living) **LANGUAGES** | **NAMES OF MAIN LANGUAGES** (speakers in population; *including second-language use) OL: official lg. | **NUMBER OF DICTIONARIES** |
|---|---|---|---|---|---|
| **Tanzania**<br>Pres. Rep., 1964 | 945<br>22.5 | 18% | 127 | kiSwahili OL (*90%)<br>English OL (*20%)<br>Sukuma (12%) | 217<br>(not listed)<br>10 |
| **Togo**<br>Pres. Rep., 1960 | 57<br>3.0 | 18% | 42 | French OL (35%) | (not listed) |
| **Tunisia**<br>Pres. Rep., 1956 | 164<br>7.5 | 42% | 11 | Arabic OL (94%) | 135 |
| **Uganda**<br>Pres. Rep., 1962 | 236<br>16.0 | 25% | 41 | luGanda (16%,*39%)<br>kiSwahili (*35%)<br>English OL (*21%) | 19<br>217<br>(not listed |
| Zaïre<br>Pres. Rep., 1960 | 2,345<br>30.9 | 45% | 212 | Lingala (*30%)<br>kiSwahili (*25%)<br>Luba (7%,*10%)<br>Kongo (6%,*8%)<br>French OL (4%) | 20<br>217<br>8<br>36<br>(not listed) |
| **Zambia**<br>Pres. Rep., 1964 | 753<br>6.9 | 50% | 37 | ciBemba (19%,*56%)<br>chiNyanja (11%,*42%)<br>English OL (*26%) | 23<br>26<br>(not listed) |
| **Zimbabwe**<br>Pres. Rep., 1980 | 391<br>8.4 | 49% | 19 | Shona (67%)<br>siNdebele (15%) | 28<br>5 |

Appendix B: **List of Contributors**

AL-BESBASI, Ibrahim [author of State-of-the-art Report on Libya]
Ph.D. student at Exeter

ALI, Abdurahman A. [author of State-of-the-art Report on Somalia]
Assistant Lexicographer, Somali Academy of Sciences and Arts, Mogadisho (Diploma Exeter 1989)

BUSANE, Masidake [author of Paper 3 and State-of-the-art Report on Zaïre]
Chef de Travaux in English, University of Lubumbashi, Zaïre (Ph.D. student at Exeter)

BWENGE, Charles Muttabazi T. [author of State-of-the-art Report on Tanzania]
Assistant Research Fellow, Institute of Kiswahili Research (TUKI), University of Dar es Salaam, Tanzania (M.Phil. Exeter 1988)

DIAB, Turki A.
Lecturer in English for Specific Purposes, University of Jordan (Ph.D. Exeter 1989)

DODD, W. Steven
Lecturer in Applied Linguistics, University of Exeter

EL-BADRY, Nawal Hamza [author of Paper 4 and State-of-the-art Report on Egypt]
Lecturer in Arabic Translation, University of Salford (Ph.D. Exeter 1990)

GOUWS, Dr. Rufus H. [author of Paper 6 and State-of-the-art Report on R.S.A.]
Lecturer in Afrikaans, University of Stellenbosch, R.S.A. (Honorary Research Fellow at Exeter 1986)

GÜNTHER, Dr. Wilfried
Lecturer in Languages, Lancashire Polytechnic, Preston (M.Phil. student at Exeter)

HARTMANN, Dr. Reinhard R.K. [author of Paper 7, Appendix A and general editor]
Director of Language Centre and Dictionary Research Centre, University of Exeter

ISKANDER, Wafaa
Tutor in Arabic, University of Exeter

KATUPHA, J.M.M. [author of State-of-the-art Report on Mozambique]
Núcleo de Estudo de Línguas Moçambicanas, Universidade Eduardo Mondlane, Maputo, Mozambique (Ph.D. student at S.O.A.S., London)

KIDDA AWAK, Dr. Mairo [author of Paper 2 and State-of-the-art Report on Nigeria]
Lecturer in Linguistics, University of Maiduguri, Nigeria (Commonwealth Fellow at Exeter 1988-89)

MANN, Michael [author of Papers 1 and 5 and State-of-the-art Reports on Djibouti, Ethiopia, and Zambia]
Lecturer in Bantu Languages, School of Oriental and African Studies, University of London

NDOMA, Dr. Ungina [author of additional references on lexicography in Zaïre]
Institute Pédagogique National at Kinshasa, Zaïre

NIKIEMA, André D. [author of State-of-the-art Report on Burkina Faso] (M.A. Exeter 1989)

ZE AMVELA, Dr. Etienne E. [author of State-of-the-art Report on Cameroon]
Deputy Director-General, University Centre of Buea, Cameroon

EXETER LINGUISTIC STUDIES

General Editor: R.R.K. Hartmann

1 A Reader on Language Variety
edited by C.S. Butler and R.R.K. Hartmann, 1976, 1979

2 The Development of Syntax in a Group of Educationally Severely Subnormal Children
by Gillian Fenn, 1977

3 Cognitive Linguistics and Social Interaction
by Robin P. Fawcett, 1980 (Heidelberg: Julius Groos Verlag)

4 Dictionaries and their Users
edited by R.R.K. Hartmann, 1979 (out of print)

5 On Idiom: critical views and perspectives
by Chitra Fernando and Roger Flavell, 1981

6 Understanding Semantics
by D. Connor Ferris, 1983

7 The ESP Classroom: methodology, materials and expectations
edited by Gregory James, 1983

8 Workbook on Lexicography
by Barbara Ann Kipfer, with Jennifer Robinson (glossary), Henri Béjoint, A.P. Cowie, R.R.K. Hartmann, Lesley Jeffries, W.J.R. Martin and N.E. Osselton (exercises), 1984

9 Language Standards and their Codification: process and application
edited by J.D. Woods, 1984

10 Language Theories of the Early Soviet Period
by K.H. Phillips, 1986

11 Communicative Language Testing
by Cyril J. Weir, 1988

12 Lexicography in China
by David Chien, 1986

13 Applied Text Linguistics
edited by Alan Turney, 1988

14 Lexicographers and their Works
edited by Gregory James, 1989

15 Lexicography in Africa. Progress Reports from the D.R.C. Workshop at Exeter, 24-25 March 1989
edited by R.R.K. Hartmann

16 Dictionary Workbooks. A Critical Evaluation
by Martin P. Stark